Francis Frederick Walrond

Christian Missions before the Reformation

Francis Frederick Walrond

Christian Missions before the Reformation

ISBN/EAN: 9783337202347

Printed in Europe, USA, Canada, Australia, Japan

Cover: Foto ©ninafisch / pixelio.de

More available books at **www.hansebooks.com**

CHRISTIAN MISSIONS

BEFORE THE

REFORMATION.

LONDON:
GILBERT AND RIVINGTON, PRINTERS,
ST. JOHN'S SQUARE.

ST. GALL DESTROYING THE IDOLS.

Frontispiece. *Page 59.*

CHRISTIAN MISSIONS

BEFORE THE

REFORMATION.

BY THE
REV. F. F. WALROND, M.A.
VICAR OF THROWLEY, KENT.

Published under the Direction of the Tract Committee.

LONDON:
SOCIETY FOR PROMOTING CHRISTIAN KNOWLEDGE;
SOLD AT THE DEPOSITORIES:
77, GREAT QUEEN STREET, LINCOLN'S INN FIELDS
4, ROYAL EXCHANGE; 48, PICCADILLY;
AND BY ALL BOOKSELLERS.

CONTENTS.

	PAGE
I. ST. PATRICK	7
II. ST. COLUMBAN	29
III. ST. GALL AND THE DISCIPLES OF COLUMBAN	57
IV. ST. BONIFACE	71
V. GREGORY AND STURM	107
VI. ANSCHAR	121
VII. TENTH CENTURY—ADALBERT OF PRAGUE	150
VIII. OTTO OF BAMBERG, APOSTLE OF POMERANIA	171

CHRISTIAN MISSIONS BEFORE THE REFORMATION.

ST. PATRICK.

So vast a mass of absurd legends, popular delusions, and apparently deliberate falsehoods, have in the course of ages clustered round the name of St. Patrick, that much time has to be spent in the clearing away of rubbish before we can lay bare anything like the true image of his life and character. When the work is done, we find revealed to us a Christian man, who, for unwavering faith, fervent love, sustained self-devotion, and sincere humility, has perhaps seldom been equalled and scarcely ever surpassed. The process reminds one of some of the excavations which are being carried on at Rome. On the surface there is perhaps a modern Church, decorated profusely with all the outward signs and symbols of a superstitious worship. Beneath it is an earlier structure, like that which met the eye at first, but with a difference, distinguished by greater simplicity and a less evident regard for outward show; while, beneath this again, unsuspected when the excavation was commenced, there is found a third, earliest of all and simplest of all, which by its mere appearance enters a silent but perpetual protest against the corruptions under which it had been hidden. Yet there is a likeness discernible through the series; the latest is the caricature of the earliest. So it has been with the history of St. Patrick. Brave and holy man, among the foremost of the soldiers of the Cross, he spent his life in doing battle for his Lord, and striking heavy blows against the world, the flesh, and the devil, and winning for Christ a land which to all appearance was a stronghold of Satan. His name lives across the ages and men call him Saint, and know that he was a blessing to mankind, but if you ask what the blessing was, and why his name is venerated, you are likely enough to be told that it is because he cleared the soil of Ireland of snakes and vermin, and drained the marshes which had brought disease and death. Or if you ask the question of another you will perhaps be told that St. Patrick brought the darkness of Popery into the land, and that therefore those who love that darkness call him a hero and honour his memory. The truth is that the snakes and vermin which he destroyed were the idols of pagan superstition, the marshes which he dried up were the bogs of unbelief, and the Popery which he is accused of bringing with him is a thing which he most likely never heard of, and certainly would have abjured if he had. Miracles of which he knew nothing, silly stories in which he never took part, homage to Rome which he never paid, have been worked together into a compact mass of fable which has disgusted men and frightened them from examining the story of his life. Among the innumerable mischiefs which Rome has done by her system of "pious fraud," not the least is this, that the bright example of holy men of old is obscured and was for ages lost to the Church.

One of these is St. Patrick. It so happens that in his case, we have a work of his own, which he addressed to his converts after he had been labouring for thirty years, and of which there is not the slightest reason to doubt the genuineness. It is called his Confessions, and it bears in its simple rude style an impress that exactly corresponds to the age and country in which it was written, and to the stage of culture of its author. It contains none of the wonderful stories which the inventors of the lives of saints invariably loved to insert into their narratives by way of glorifying their hero. And this alone makes it impossible to believe that it was written in a later age and by another hand. There are to be found in it none of the traditions which appeared after the lapse of centuries respecting him, and which his own biographer, Jocelin, who lived in the twelfth century, is careful to pass on. In fact there is no pretence of miracle or wonder in the book, except so far as all the ways of Divine Providence must needs be wonderful, all supernatural.

If ever man was marked out by Divine Providence for a particular work, and trained and prepared for it by the events of his early years and the peculiar trials and sufferings which he was made to undergo, Patrick would seem to have been such a man. He was born about the year 372, at the village of Bonaven, now called Kil-Patrick, on the north bank of the river Clyde, between Glasgow and Dumbarton. This district was then the borderland between comparative light and darkness. To the north was barbarism, to the south the light of the Gospel, and the latter was gradually bringing in its train that civilization which is always sure, sooner or later, to follow it. So the dawn was gradually creeping northwards. But there was no sign as yet of the present divisions of the country. There was no England and there was no Scotland. The nations had scarcely even begun the slow process of settling down into definite form. Meanwhile it was a time of tumult and fear. The Picts and Scots in the North were perpetually making incursions into the South and carrying off men, women, and property. The Scots, from whom Scotland afterwards took its name, had as yet crossed from Ireland, their former home, only in occasional bands of robbers and pirates, spreading terror wherever they appeared. And in the midst of this, and in the daily sight or fear of it, Patrick's early years were passed. He was the son of a priest named Calphornius, a man of some note and influence, who himself was the son of Olid, a deacon, so that Patrick was of an ecclesiastical family, and likely to receive at least as good an education as any other boy of his years; but no great amount of learning was to be had in those days in out-of-the-way places. Still he seems to have received his fair share of instruction; he was taught the doctrines of Christianity, and, perhaps, had a smattering of such other teaching as was within reach; but till his seventeenth year he led a thoughtless boyish life, with no very distinct aim or purpose in his mind. The head-knowledge of the Gospel which had been imparted to him was a treasure of which he had not yet learned the value. The time was coming now when he would be forced to turn it over and over; the truth was to find its way from his head to his heart, and become a living thing and life-giving. His heavenly Father sent him a severe chastisement to awake him from the sleep of death to a higher life. The daily fear came closer to his own home and became an actual fact. A band of Scottish pirates from Ireland sailed up the Clyde, and landed near Bonaven, and among others Patrick himself, now sixteen, was carried away captive to the district called Dalaradia, in the north of Ireland, and there sold as a slave to a pagan chieftain, named Milcho. His employment [was to take care of his master's flocks of sheep. This compelled him to spend much time alone in the open air, and solitude became pleasant to him. Words which he had been taught in his father's house came back to his memory now with power to support and save. Trouble led his heart to God, Whom in the quiet days which were passed he had forgotten. Forsaken by men, he found in Him consolation and joy, and now first learned to know the meaning of a treasure in heaven that faileth not. He wandered about with his flocks in the ice and snow, but in his heart he began to hold communion with God in prayer and meditation. He speaks of all this himself in his Confessions. " I was about sixteen years old, and I knew not the true God, and I and many thousand persons were carried into captivity into a strange land. We were recompensed herein according to our deserts, for we had departed from God and not kept His commandments. But God opened my unbelieving mind, so that, late as it was, I began to think of my sin, and turned with my whole heart to the Lord my God. He had looked down on my low condition, had had pity on my youth and ignorance, and before I knew Him, before I could distinguish between good and evil, He had guarded, protected, and cherished me as a father doth his son. This I know, that before God humbled me I was like a stone sunk in the mire; but when He came Who had power to do it, He raised me in

His mercy, and set me in a very high place." "When I was brought to Ireland, and had daily charge of the cattle, I prayed many times in the day; the fear of God and the love of Him were kindled in me more and more; faith increased in me, so that in one day I prayed a hundred times, and at night almost as many; and when I passed a night in the woods or on the mountains, I rose up to pray in the snow, ice, and rain, before daybreak. Yet I felt no pain; there was no sluggishness in me, such as I now find in myself, for then the spirit glowed within me."

After he had been six years in Milcho's service he twice had a dream, in which he heard a voice bidding him fly to the sea-coast, where he would find a ship ready to take him and convey him back to his native country. The dream was probably nothing but the echo of his waking thoughts, but in dependence on this call he set out, and after a journey of several days he met with a vessel which was on the point of sailing. The captain refused to receive the poor unknown youth, and Patrick went away, fell on his knees, and prayed. He had not finished his prayer when one of the ship's company called him back; the captain had changed his mind. After undergoing many sufferings and being mercifully preserved from great dangers, he reached home once more. Ten years afterwards he was a second time taken captive by Scottish freebooters, and conveyed this time to Gaul. But after sixty days a special interposition of Providence, by means of Christian merchants, restored him to liberty, and once more he returned home. He might now have lived quietly with his friends, who entreated him not again to venture away from his home. But he felt an irresistible impulse to carry the message of salvation to the people among whom he had passed his youth, and the country where he had himself been born, again to the life of heaven. And again his waking thoughts were reflected in his dreams. He thought he saw a man named Victricius, coming as if from Ireland with a vast number of letters. He gave him one of them. It was headed with the words, "The voice of the Irish." While he was reading the letter he heard the Irish who dwelt in the wood Foclut, near the sea, calling to him with one voice, "We beseech thee, child of God, come again and walk among us." Another night he heard in a dream a voice from heaven, crying," He Who gave His life for thee, He speaks in thee." One night it was as if there was something in him, and yet above him, which was not himself, praying with deep sighs; and at the close of the prayer it spoke as if it were no other than the Spirit of God. And he awoke and remembered the words, " The Spirit helpeth our infirmities; for we know not what we should pray for as we ought, but the Spirit itself maketh intercession for us with groanings which cannot be uttered." These dreams made him more determined than ever to accomplish his purpose. His friends could not understand him, and with tears entreated him to remain at home. " But against my wishes," he says, "I was forced to offend my relations, and many of those who wished me well. It was not in my own power, but it was God Who conquered in me and withstood them all; so that I went to the people of Ireland to preach the Gospel, and suffered many insults from unbelievers, and many persecutions, even unto bonds, giving up my liberty that I might be made a blessing to others. And if I am found worthy I am ready to give up my life with joy for His Name's sake."

But he would not rush suddenly and unprepared into the responsibilities and difficulties of such a work. He went first to Gaul, and spent four years in the monastery lately founded by St. Martin at

Tours. He also studied with St. Germain of Auxerre, under whose direction he acquired a knowledge of "the ecclesiastical canons, and served God in labours, in fastings, in chastity of life, in contrition of heart, and in the love of God and of his neighbour."

The old legends relate that he next made a journey to Rome, in order to receive full powers and consecration to his office from the Roman Bishop. The Archdeacon Palladius had been sent from Rome as a missionary to Ireland, but being ignorant of the language, he had accomplished little or nothing. The news of his death had just arrived when Patrick reached Rome, and Pope Sixtus III. at once appointed him to the vacant place. So says the story. It is wholly destitute of historical support, and is beset with difficulties. The Irish Church from its commencement exhibits a spirit of antagonism, not of subservience to Rome, and there is none of that similarity in ecclesiastical usages which never failed to exist in Churches which really did owe their foundation to the Church of Rome. Moreover Patrick himself, in his Confessions, gives no indication whatever of any commission received from the Pope, but, on the contrary, everything favours the supposition that he was ordained Bishop in Britain itself. The story is of a kind which was only too common half a dozen centuries after Patrick's time, and is to be put on a level with the false decretals and other inventions by which Rome established her ascendency.

At length Patrick landed in Ireland, accompanied by a small band of priests and deacons who had been ordained with him. He landed at the place now occupied by the town of Wicklow, but, after a brief sojourn in that district, hastened northwards towards the home of his old master Milcho, whom he wished to make the firstfruits of his preaching. Another chieftain, however, Sinell, son of Finnehad, was the first of the Irish whom he baptized; and he also, on the way, converted Dicho, another chief, who bestowed upon him, as a site for a church, the place on which his barn was erected. It was named Sabhul Padruig, "the barn of Patrick," and its ruins are still to be seen at Saul, in the county of Down. Dicho remained a steady friend of Patrick for the rest of his life, and Saul became his favourite retreat in his latter days. He devoted himself particularly to win over the chiefs to the faith; while they remained under the influence of the Druids they might do much harm among their followers; and their superior education made it sometimes more easy to convince them of the absurdity of idolatry. Indeed, some of them were already longing to hear the Word of God. It is recorded of Cormac, an Irish prince, who must have lived a short time before the coming of Patrick, that he abdicated his government, and gave himself up in solitude to silent reflection and religious contemplation, and in this way to have attained to a conviction of the vanity of what the Druids taught. To minds such as this " the Word of the truth of the Gospel " must have been as a refreshing rain.

Patrick was at one time in a family of rank, the members of which he baptized. The son of the house, a youth, was so fascinated by his bearing and his words that, in spite of the persuasion of his friends, he resolved to forsake all and follow him in all his dangers and toils. On account of his friendly, gentle disposition, Patrick gave him the name of Benignus. He was gifted with a fine musical voice, and his singing was of great service in winning the attention of the people, among whom he continued zealously labouring till his death, having succeeded Patrick in the pastoral office and the see of Armagh. The knowledge which Patrick had obtained of the Irish language in the days of his slavery was his most valuable means of usefulness now. He assembled round him in the open fields, at the sound of a drum, large assemblies of people, and told them of the love of the Saviour for sinful men, and the word of the Cross evinced its power on the hearts of multitudes. He met, indeed, with warm opposition. The priests and national bards had great influence, and they instigated the people against him, so that he had to endure many severe persecutions. But his faith, and zeal, and love were victorious; many of the bards were themselves converted, and sang in their own hymns the vanity of idolatry and the praises of God and Christ. He frequently travelled round the whole island, accompanied by his pupils, and read to the people out of the Gospels, and preached on what he had read. Sometimes, however, for a considerable length of time together, he fixed his head-quarters at one place. At first this place was the residence of Dicho, but about Easter in the next year he changed the scene of his labours in order to visit Tara, which was then the capital of Ireland.

Tara, or Temora, was situated in what is now the county of Meath, and had been a royal residence from the most remote antiquity. It was one of those ancient centres round which, among a barbarous or semi-civilized people, myths and traditions love to cluster; and it was the stronghold of paganism and superstition at the time when Patrick went there to endeavour to convert the kings and chieftains of Ireland. It was Easter Eve when Patrick, coming from Ulster, arrived at the place called in the Irish language Ferta-fir-feic, or "The graves of the men of Feic." Here he resolved to pass the night, and his companions lighted a fire to prepare their food. But it happened that the Irish chieftains were just then assembled to celebrate one of their religious festivals; and it was the privilege of Tara that none should presume to light a fire in Ireland that day until the sacred fire had been first lighted for the festival. This privilege Patrick had ignorantly violated; and when Leogaire, the Irish monarch, was made aware of what had happened, he was filled with superstitious terror, and he was still more alarmed when he was urged by the Druids to seize the offender and put him to death, for if the fire were not extinguished by sunset, whoever had lighted it would become sovereign of Ireland. Wild with superstitious dread, both of the Druids and of the unknown intruder, Leogaire made some few feeble efforts to accomplish the destruction of the latter; but they were ineffectual, and at last he relented and invited the dangerous stranger to the palace of Tara. Patrick immediately accepted the invitation, and with eight companions, including Benignus, he presented himself at the palace on the following day, Easter Sunday. It was a rare opportunity for impressing the minds of exactly those persons whom he was most anxious to win for the Kingdom of God, and he was not the man to neglect it. The Druids were present and opposed him with all their might; but his preaching of the Gospel was followed by a rich harvest of converts. Among them it is said that Leogaire himself was included, as well as one of the most celebrated bards.

Patrick continued for some time to reside at Tara, and many converts were added to the Church. Among these were some of high rank and great wealth, who were liberal in their donations of land and money. Thus Conall, a brother of King Leogaire, gave the ground on which his own hall stood as a site for a church, and Enda, another brother, dedicated his infant son to a religious life, and gave up for the service of religion the ninth part of all his lands and farms. The lands which he received as presents from converted chieftains Patrick applied to the founding of cloisters. He had already seen in France, and to a certain extent, no doubt, in Britain, that whatever might be the peculiar dangers and temptations of the monastic life, yet in those days monasteries were almost the only means of opposing the inroads of barbarism; they were like fortresses of the Gospel, round which the waves of pagan idolatry might sweep again and again, but from which the messengers of Christ might as often sally forth to bless the land. The cloisters were nursing-schools for teachers of the people, and from them was to proceed the civilization of the country. It was not in Patrick's own power, indeed, to impart much scientific instruction to his monks, but he started them in the right direction, and inspired them with that love of learning which afterwards sent them to seek for more information, and for books, in Britain, France, and Italy. And in another way, also, they were indebted to him for a gift which was the foundation of all future progress, for he invented an alphabet for the Irish language.

In all that he did, and in every moment of every

day, he relied upon the constant guidance and support of that God Whose Word he was engaged in publishing. His letters and Confessions are full of the sense of his own unworthiness and weakness, and also of the consciousness of the power and grace of God that worked in him and by him. Coupled with this he had the strongest conviction that he was sent by God for the express purpose of carrying the Gospel to the Irish people, and that the work which was given him to do upon earth was to give to them the gift of eternal life. He had a yearning desire to revisit his native land, and to see once more his relatives and friends in Britain and Gaul, but this desire was sacrificed to the furtherance of the one object of his life. " God knows," he says, "that I earnestly wish it; but I am bound by the Spirit, who testifies that He will pronounce me guilty if I do this, and I dread lest the work I have begun should fall to the ground. I pray God that He may grant me perseverance to enable me to approve myself a faithful witness, for the sake of my God, to the end. And if I have ever laboured to accomplish anything good for the sake of my God Whom I love, may He grant that, with those converts and captives of mine, I may pour out my blood for His name."

He had much to bear continually from the opposition of the pagan chiefs. Once, when on a journey, he was set upon by one of them, robbed, put in chains, and thrown into prison. He was not released for fourteen days. Nor was it only with Irish pagans that he had to contend. Once a pirate chief from Wallia, or Wales, landed upon the coast and fell upon a number of persons who had been recently baptized, and after murdering some of them carried off the rest to sell them as slaves to the Picts and Scots. The chief, whose name was Carodac, was a professing Christian. The letter which Patrick in his indignation wrote on this occasion is still preserved. He pronounces all Christians implicated in the transaction to be excommunicated, and forbids any one to eat or drink in their company, until, with many tears and sincere repentance, they atoned for their crimes, and set at liberty the servants and handmaids of God, for whom Christ died and was crucified.

He always endeavoured to avoid even the semblance of seeking his own honour or profit. When many persons, full of gratitude and love to him as their spiritual father, brought him presents of their own accord, and pious women eagerly contributed their ornaments for the purpose, he was so determined to avoid all appearance of evil, that he refused them all, at the risk of offending the givers. On the other hand he was continually redeeming Christians from slavery, and was ready to give up all, even his own life, as a good shepherd for his sheep. Let us conclude our notice of him with some of his own words, taken from his Confessions. "In order that you may give me joy, and that I may give you joy in the Lord, I do not repent of what I have done, and yet it is not enough for me. I give up, and will give up, far more. The Lord is able to grant that I may give myself up for your souls. I call God to witness that I do not write this to gain honour from you. That honour is enough for me that no eye can see but which the heart believes. God is faithful. He promises and cannot deceive. But already in this world the Lord has exalted me beyond measure. I know very well that poverty and hardships are better for me than riches and a life of pleasure. Yea; even Christ the Lord became poor for our sakes. Daily I have expected to be seized, to be carried off as a slave, or to be killed. But none of all these things moved me, for I have cast myself into the arms of Almighty

God Who rules over all, as it is said, 'Cast thy burden on the Lord and He shall sustain thee.' Now I commend my soul to my faithful God Whose messenger I am; and since He is no respecter of persons, and has chosen me to this calling that I should serve Him as one of the least of His servants, how can I repay the Lord for all the goodness He has shown me? What shall I say unto my Lord, or what shall I promise Him? For I have no strength except what comes from Him. But He searches the heart and tries the reins, and He knows how greatly I desire that He would give me to drink the cup of suffering as He has given it to others who love Him. May my God never suffer me to lose by my neglect this Church which He has won in the most remote corner of the earth. I pray God that He will grant me grace to persevere, and that He will count me worthy to bear a faithful testimony until the time when I depart hence; and I beseech Him that I may be allowed to shed my blood for His name with these my converts, even though I should be allowed no burial, or my body should be torn to pieces by wild beasts. I firmly believe that, should this be my lot, my soul would be saved, and my body also; for most surely in that day we shall rise again with the brightness of the sun, that is, with the glory of our Redeemer Jesus Christ, the Son of the living God, for we are fellow-heirs with Christ, and shall be made like unto Him; He has made us kings, and we shall reign by Him, and through Him, and with Him. That sun which we see in the sky rises for us every day by God's command, but it is no living king, nor will its brightness endure for ever. All those unhappy ones who worship it shall be punished. But we adore in faith the true and living Sun, Christ, Who will never set. And he too who does His will shall never set, but will live for ever, as Christ lives for ever, and reigns with God the Father Almighty, and with the Holy Ghost from eternity, both now and for ever."

In his old age St. Patrick appears to have ceased in a measure from more arduous labours, and to have employed himself in holding Synods for the settlement of the Church. Several of the canons enacted in these councils are still in existence, and they serve to throw light upon many of the doctrines and customs of the early Irish Church. Whatever time he could secure from these engagements he passed in retirement at Saul, where, in prayer and meditation, he ended his days. He was buried near the site of the present Cathedral of Down.

ST. COLUMBAN.

St. Patrick had brought to Ireland a fire which could not easily be quenched, and the hearts of many were stirred to imitate his bright example. When he died, Benignus succeeded him as second Archbishop of Armagh, and continued with zeal and energy the work which had been begun by his great predecessor. One after another quickly caught the inspiration until, within a century of St. Patrick's death, the wild parts of Ireland were covered with monasteries erected by the hard labour of monks. Monasteries in those days, we must carefully remember, were not the abodes of indolence and sin which many of them only too truly became in later ages; rather they were strongholds of light and truth, fortresses in which Christian love and Christian learning kept themselves safe amid the habitations of cruelty, sallying forth as occasion offered to spread blessings round, with "power on the dark land to lighten it, and power on the dead world to make it live." And the Irish monasteries quickly became known in Europe for the strict Christian discipline which ruled in them, for the industry and perseverance with which their inmates subdued the earth and cultivated it, turning bogs into pastures, and wildernesses into fruitful fields. They became known, too, for the simple piety and earnestness which marked them, for the zeal with which the Scriptures were studied, and the efforts which were made there to acquire all such knowledge as the age could afford. Books were eagerly collected wherever they could be found. It very seldom happened that all the members of a monastic institution were entirely stationary. Some of them were nearly always engaged in foreign travel. The love of travel, which we so often hear spoken of as characteristic of the English of the present day, was at least equally strong in the Irish of thirteen centuries ago. An old chronicler, referring to that period, speaks of "the Irish nation in whom the love of wandering in foreign parts has now become almost a second nature." The absence of our modern facilities of locomotion was no hindrance to them; it only offered an additional charm to an adventurous disposition. And a monk who travelled abroad seldom failed on his return to bring with him some precious volume picked up in foreign parts to enrich the library of the monastery at home.

In this way knowledge increased, and the fruits of faith became abundantly visible in the activity of a Christian life, and Ireland rapidly began to deserve the title which was afterwards given to it of "The Island of Saints." The Gospel being firmly planted in this far away island of the West, it was time that Ireland should begin to repay the great debt, and become in her turn a preacher of the kingdom of God. Those in whom the love of travel, the spirit of enterprise, the eagerness for adventure, and the ardour of Christian zeal were combining to draw them from their native land seemed marked out by Providence to be the missionaries of the world. The claim was felt and nobly answered. Missionary schools were formed in which men were expressly trained and prepared to become teachers of the heathen. The most famous of these schools was the monastery of Bangor, in the county of Down, founded soon after the middle of the sixth century by the venerable Abbot Comgal; and from this time forward an almost continuous stream of Christian men began to flow from Ireland and to freshen

Britain and the Continent with the water of life. First went forth Columba to preach the Gospel among the Northern Picts, those same heathen who had been the terror of the boyhood of St. Patrick, and who were separated by the snowy range of the Grampians from civilization and the knowledge of Christ. Every one has heard of Columba's monastery of Iona, the ruins of which are still to be seen, and from which the light shone through the North of Scotland, and eventually through the North of England also; for Iona was the spiritual parent of Holy Island and of the Church of Durham.

Some twenty-five years afterwards the example of Columba was followed by Columban. He was born in the year 560, in the province of Leinster. A youth of a comely, graceful, person and attractive manners, he had added to these the accomplishments of the age; he learnt the liberal arts, grammar, rhetoric, and geometry. But very early in life he became the subject of deep religious impressions, and, fearing lest his natural advantages might become a snare to him, he travelled into another part of Ireland and put himself under the guidance of a venerable Christian teacher named Silen, and devoted himself entirely to the study of sacred literature. Afterwards he entered the monastery of Bangor, where he remained till the age of thirty. Then came the Divine call from above; he felt powerfully the true missionary impulse, the longing kindled by the fire of the Lord to go forth and preach the Gospel to the nations sitting in darkness. His pupil Jonas, who also became his biographer, gives the words in which he spoke of himself at this time:—

"Oh that God would grant to me—for lowly as I am, I am still His servant indeed—that I might be roused from my sleep of indolence, and the fire of Divine love kindled within me and for ever kept burning! Oh that I had the true fuel with which that fire might be perpetually fed and never be quenched, but increase for ever more and more! Give me, I pray Thee, O Lord, in the name of Jesus Christ, Thy Son, my God, that undying love which will kindle my lamp and not extinguish it, so that it may burn on in me and be a light to others also. Do Thou Thyself, O Christ our Saviour, kindle our lamps, that they may evermore shine in Thy Temple; that the light which welleth forth from Thee may shine into the darkness of our hearts, and make through us the darkness of the world less deep. Give me Thine own light,

O Jesus, I pray Thee, that my eyes may look upon that Holy of Holies where Thou dwellest, the eternal Priest, that I may always behold Thee, desire Thee, gaze upon Thee, and long after Thee. Thine it is, O Saviour full of love, to show Thyself to us, that we may know Thee, love Thee alone, think of Thee alone day and night; that Thy love may fill our souls, and that this mighty love may never more be quenched by the waters of this world, as it is written, 'Many waters cannot quench love.'"

When Columban expressed his desire to his Abbot, the latter for some time refused his permission, not willing to allow himself to be deprived of so useful an assistant, but at last he was convinced that it was God's will, and gave his consent; and in 590 Columban set sail with twelve youths, whom the Abbot gave him to be his companions, and to be trained under his spiritual guidance. He landed in the kingdom of the Franks, and his intention was to pass through it and preach the Gospel to the heathen tribes dwelling on its borders. But the fame of his piety reached the ears of one of the kings of the land, and he was intreated to take up his residence within the empire itself. It was a country which ought to have been Christian, and was so in name; but the violence of human passions, and the devastations of perpetual wars had brought back to desolation and barbarism what had once been a smiling and cultivated region. The sites of ancient towns were now in many cases savage wildernesses. Columban purposely sought out one of these centres of devastation; he was determined to find a spot which must first be reclaimed and rendered habitable by severe labour. He was anxious for the sake of his monks themselves that at the very outset they should learn self-denial by the overcoming of difficulty, and acquire hardness and self-control by doing wholly without the comforts of this life; and, for the sake of the barbarous people around, he wished to set an example of tilling and subduing the earth, and so make a beginning of social improvement. But the most extraordinary exertions were required for them to supply themselves with even the most necessary means of living. Until the soil was rendered fruitful and began to supply them with food, they subsisted almost entirely upon herbs and the bark of trees, with whatever fish they could catch in the mountain streams. The place where they first settled was among the ruins of an ancient town called Anegratis, now

Anegrey, in a forest of the Vosges mountains. Columban kept his monks steadily employed in the most active labours for their own support; but even when human means of sustenance seemed most precarious, he relied with unwavering confidence on the providence of God. Sometimes he was delivered from the most extreme distress by a sudden and unforeseen combination of circumstances, and each occasion of this kind strengthened the confidence of his companions, and caused him to be regarded by the people around as a favourite of heaven. At one time, when the monks were vainly endeavouring to satisfy their hunger with herbs and the bark of trees, one of their number, to make matters worse, was taken ill, and they had no means of tending him. When they had spent three days in apparently unavailing prayer for their sick brother, a man suddenly appeared at the convent door with horses laden with sacks of provisions. All he could say was, that a sudden impulse had seized him which he could not resist, to bring help to those who were suffering in the wilderness for Christ's sake. Another time, after nine days of similar privation, provisions were sent them in a like unexpected manner. Once a foreign priest visited them, and went with Columban to look at the store of grain which they happened at that time to have laid up. The visitor expressed his surprise that so small a store would suffice for the wants of so many; but Columban replied, "If men will only serve God with all their hearts, this in itself exempts them from the danger of starvation. It is written in the thirty-seventh Psalm, 'I have never seen the righteous forsaken, nor his seed begging their bread.' He Who once with five loaves of bread satisfied five thousand can easily fill our barns with corn." In all this we see no overstrained reliance upon miracle or expectation of miraculous help; only a healthy and vigorous faith which trusts in the providence of God working by natural means.

In the midst of his great activity in the outer life Columban proved his Christian simplicity, and the repose of his soul in God, by the delight which he took in religious contemplation and inward quiet. He was frequently seen to retire into the depths of the forest, carrying a Bible on his shoulder. He read as he walked, and meditated on what he read, or sat down with the Bible in his hand on the trunk of a tree in solitude. On Sundays and feast days he delighted to retire to a cave or any secret place where he could be alone, and give himself up entirely to prayer and meditation on Divine things. Such caves are abundant in that country. Those who have had the good fortune to travel among the Vosges mountains cannot have forgotten the strange and often very beautiful character of the scenery. The outline of the hills is usually round and tame, broken here and there by bold escarpments of the old red sandstone, constrasting beautifully in colour with the dense green foliage of the forest from the midst of which they project. These rocky headlands are frequently crowned by the remains of castles more or less completely ruined, the strongholds of predatory chieftains during the middle ages, and the successors of robber fastnesses of the time of Columban. But the range presents great diversity of scenery; here rising in irregular though rounded heights, there sinking in easy undulations to the plain below, desolate then, but now rich and cultivated; here swelling in wooded slopes, and there retiring in winding glens or rounded valley basins. A few miles' walk into this district would bring the lover of solitude into scenes where no human voice would be likely to disturb his prayer. And here on Sundays and feast days Columban used to retire from the strife of tongues, when the duties of his convent would allow, and lay up stores of strength in prayer and meditation, for a renewed conflict with the wild passions of men in the week days which were coming. He was "with the wild beasts;" wolves and bears watched him as he passed, but he did not come to injure them, and they never did him harm.

But every day that passed left him less and less alone. More and more the cares of his convent increased as the convent itself grew larger in size, and the necessity of perpetual action and perpetual counsel and command left him less and less time for quiet meditation; while, on the other hand, those who had followed him when he left his home were catching more and more of his spirit, entering more and more into the holy hope and purpose of his life, and were more and more able and ready to help him in the work which lay before them all. Far and wide too the example which he was setting, and the mode of life which he was living, became known and talked of; men spoke of him with wonder and admiration, and the loftiness of his spirit fascinated and attracted multitudes who were not themselves prepared to soar to such a height. But many did put their hands to the plough, and though some looked backward, great numbers endured to the end. Families of every rank committed their sons to him for education. Morally, spiritually, socially, intellectually, as well as in the outward aspect of the soil he was tilling, he deeply set his mark upon the people and the land.

His convent had already far outgrown his original plan, and the slender accommodation of the ruins of Anegratis became quite inadequate for the reception of the daily increasing numbers who continued to flock to him. What was he to do? He dared not turn away those who came to him to be taught the life of God. But his little kingdom had already become unwieldy. To enlarge its borders would only relax its discipline, and open the door to confusion and disorder. Another colony must be founded in some other spot; another rivet made fast, to hold the land for God. Ruins in those unhappy times were never far to seek; ruins where any man might dwell, who could keep the wild beasts and the robbers at bay. About eight miles from Anegratis were the ruins of a more extensive and more pretentious town. The Romans, in the days of their power, had chosen a strong position, and fortified it strongly, and called it Luxuvium, the modern Luxeuil, in Franche Comté, in what is now the Department of the Upper Saône. In the times of its prosperity it was celebrated for its warm springs, and while the Roman rule was still able to enforce order, and protect life and property, it continued to be a favourite place of residence. Splendid baths, temples, and other stately buildings rose with all the grandeur which usually characterized a wealthy provincial town. But its glory has passed away. Its remains were now overgrown with the wild forest jungle. But Columban's biographer, Jonas, tells us, that in his time, the woods around were still thickly strewn with marble statues and other magnificent vestiges of the old Pagan idolatry. Columban determined to take possession of these ruins, and consecrate the spot to be the site of a new monastery, larger and more perfect than Anegratis. But with new and increased accommodation came new and increasing claims. The stream continued to flow, and once more there was found to be no room for the numbers of those who sought shelter in the holy retreat. Another spot must be discovered, another colony established. True to his original plan of compelling his followers to test their resolution by severe toil and hard labour for the means of life, Columban once more selected a spot in the very thickest of the forest, beautiful indeed and charming to the eye, but where roots and the bark of trees, and such fish as the mountain streams might supply, would be their only sustenance, until they could subdue the earth, and raise crops from the soil. The place derived its name from the unusual number of streams by which it was watered; and here in time rose the Abbey of Fontaines.

Columban presided as Abbot over the whole cluster of religious communities. His delight was still to wander alone in the woods, in reading, meditation, and prayer, but such opportunities had now become rare. He exercised strict superintendence over all the monasteries of his rule, and he took part in their labours, and helped them with example so wise, and counsel so unerring, that men said to one another that he must be guided by inspiration from above.

Now that Columban's spiritual family had become so large, and separated into such distinct portions, it became necessary to supply them with some common rule according to which their daily common life should be ordered, and each individual trained to take his proper part in the work of the whole body. It was perhaps about the time of the foundation of Fontaines that he wrote his "Instructiones Variæ," or Instructions for the guidance of his monks. His one object in all his monastic regulations was to accustom to self-denial, or the total surrender of the will to God, those who were placed under his guidance. "Whoever overcomes himself," he says, "treads the world underfoot. No one who spares himself can hate the world. It is in the inmost soul that one either loves or hates the world." Again, "We must willingly surrender for Christ's sake all that we love out of Christ. First of all, if we are called to do so, we must give up our bodily life in martyrdom for Christ. Or if we are not called to this, our will must still be completely mortified; so that they who live should not henceforth live unto themselves, but unto Him Who died for them. Let us therefore live to Him, Who, though He died for us, is our life; let us die to ourselves that we may live to Christ. For we cannot live to Him, if we do not first die to ourselves: let us be Christ's, not our own, for we are bought with a price; the Master gave Himself for the servant, the King for his attendants, God for man. Let us therefore die for life, since He Who is the life died for the dead, that we too may be able to say, 'I live, yet not I, but Christ liveth in me;' this is the language of the chosen. No one can die to himself, if Christ does not live in him; but if Christ be in him, he cannot live to himself. Live then in Christ that Christ may live in thee. We must take the kingdom of heaven by violence, for we have to fight not only with our enemies, but still more earnestly with ourselves. It is a grievous misery for a man to injure himself and not to know it. If thou hast conquered thyself thou hast conquered all things." Again, " It becomes travellers to hasten towards their home. As long as they are on their journey they are full of care; when they reach their home, they are at rest. Let us, then, who are travelling, hasten to our native country, for all our life is but like a day's journey. The first thing for us is to love nothing here below, but to love only what is above; to long only after what is above; to think only of that; to seek only our fatherland above, there where our Father is. Here on earth we have not our fatherland, because our Father is in heaven."

This spirit of Christian self-denial, combined with

love, was the spirit which habitually actuated Columban himself, and which he earnestly and unceasingly endeavoured to impart to his monks. But his task was difficult indeed. The twelve whom he had brought with him from Ireland had, indeed, been accustomed in some degree from their youth to rule and regular discipline; but the multitudes who joined him in France had now for the first time to be reduced to subjection, to be rescued from their wild and licentious habits, to be trained to a life of industry, to the endurance of difficulties and privations, and the submission of the flesh to the spirit. We ought not to wonder if, with such a task before him, he sometimes erred just a little on the side of strictness. He saw plainly enough that self-will is the root of all evil, and that obedience is the very foundation of good, and he was certainly led on, not to exaggerate this principle, for that is impossible, but to apply it somewhat erroneously. Obedience is a Divine thing when it means the free and hearty submission of the will to God, but if it means the surrender of the will in slavish subjection to the will of another, then it is in direct contradiction to the liberty with which Christ has made us free. It cannot be denied that Columban on this point made a mistake. We see in him already the beginning of the monastic spirit by which obedience was turned into an idol, to be worshipped for its own sake. In each of his monasteries he enforced the most entire subjection to the will of the Superior, and he even taught that the monk who simply obeyed fulfilled by that obedience the duties of his calling; if the thing done were sinful, the blame would rest not on him, but entirely on the Superior who gave the order. But whatever might be the later corruptions and exaggerations of this doctrine, it is easy to see that to Columban it appeared solely as a help to a holy life. "If the monks," he says, "learn the humility of Christ, His yoke will be easy, His burden will be light. Heart-humbleness is the repose of a soul wearied by its conflict with corrupt inclinations, and inward pain; it is its only refuge from so many evils, and the more completely it collects itself into this state from the perpetual distraction of outward vanities, so much more perfect is its repose and inward refreshment, so that even the bitter is sweet, and what before was too hard or too heavy for it to bear, has now become light and easy."

Columban was very far from making the

grievous mistake which was already common in the Church, of supposing that bodily austerities were of themselves profitable and even meritorious. He looked upon all outward things solely as means to help the growth of inward holiness. "Let the monk," he says in his Instructions, "live in a convent under the discipline of a father, and in fellowship with many others, that from the former he may learn humility, and by means of the latter patience; by the one he may learn silent obedience, by the other gentleness; let him not do his own will, let him eat only what is offered him, and have only what is given him; let him daily do the work marked out for the day. Let him go to bed weary, let him learn to take his rest even while travelling, and let him be often compelled to get up though he has not slept enough. When he suffers unjustly, let him be silent. Let him fear his Superior as a master and love him as a father."

This fear and love were exactly what Columban had succeeded in leading his monks to feel towards himself. They looked upon him as a strict and loving father. If he was stern to them, they knew very well that he was still more stern to himself. Neither towards himself nor towards them did he ever give way to a spirit of weak indulgence. Hence his influence over them was unbounded. A single word availed to make them attempt impossibilities. Once he had snatched an opportunity to retire into solitude for a little while, when news came from Luxeuil that disease had broken out in the monastery, and was spreading so rapidly that scarcely a sufficient number continued well to wait upon the sick. Instantly he was on his way, and when he arrived at Luxeuil he found that the report was only too true, the disease had spread still farther, and scarcely one remained in health. His coming brought sunshine, but not in the way they expected. Not a word of lamentation or expression of sympathy. He calmly looked round upon the invalids and said, " You appear to have much corn still unthreshed in the granary there, suppose you rise and thresh it now." They looked one upon another in astonishment. One by one, however, they yielded to the authority which never failed to sway them, and they rose and went to work. Very soon he stopped them, " Your bodies are exhausted with disease, take a little refreshment." Food was placed before them, and they felt the glow of returning health. His word had roused them, his sympathy had cheered them, his wisdom had healed them. But only one who was loved and honoured like him could have done as much.

And so the months and years went by, and Columban's little army was becoming disciplined, and the land was being won for Christ. It was the only way in which it could be won. Single preachers scattered broadcast over the land could have effected nothing, even if Columban had had such preachers to send; but these monasteries were little handfuls of leaven which were already beginning to leaven the whole lump.

Twelve years passed in peace and quietness, and no one interfered with Columban in his work. The churches which had long ago been in existence in the Frankish empire knew well what he was doing, but they did not choose either to take part in it or to hinder it. They had not themselves cared for the heathen upon their border, but they were willing enough that he should care for them, and were content to let him alone. But if a man's life is pitched upon a high level, his mere existence becomes irritating to those whom his example condemns. Though he says not a word, his every action is a rebuke and a provocation. Columban could not fail to make enemies, and many of them; and as time went on whispers began to be louder and more frequent, and men shook their heads as they hinted that strange things were being done in those monasteries in the Vosges. Columban must be a heretic. At all events, some one who had lately passed that way at Easter time, when they ought to be feasting, found the community still fasting and calling it Lent. What could it mean? It meant that Columban, who had been brought up in the Irish Church, had brought with him some of its customs, and these differed from the Roman usages which were prevalent among the Franks. One of these referred to the time of keeping Easter. The British, and afterwards the Irish Churches were Quartodecimans, i. e. they calculated Easter according to the original day of the Passover Feast, the 14th of Nisan. This custom had been prevalent in the greater part of the Eastern Church, who quoted for it the authority of St. John; and it was not yet quite superseded by our present mode of calculation, which had been adopted at the Council of Nicæa. If, therefore, Christians from Ireland and from Gaul happened to be thrown together at this time of year, the contrast of usage would be striking: the one might be fasting for the Passion of our Lord, while the other was feasting for His Resurrection.

This was a difference which the authorities of the Frankish Church would not tolerate. After much disputing, a synod was held to deliberate upon the matter, and Columban was arraigned before it. It was the first synod which had been held in those parts for many years, and Columban thanked God for the sign of possibly returning life in the Church, even though the synod was held to condemn himself; and he prayed that even on this occasion they might not separate without dealing with more important matters of faith and practice. He did not appear in person, but he wrote a letter to the synod—a letter in his own style, full of sternness as well as love. He asserted plainly that if they did not show by their lives that they had heard the voice of the true Shepherd, and were following Him, they could not expect that words which they uttered only as hirelings would meet with obedience. So far as he himself was concerned, he pleads, "I am not the author of this difference. I came as a stranger to this land for the sake of our common Lord and Saviour Christ. I beseech you by that common Lord, Who shall judge us all, to allow me to live in silence, in peace, and in charity, as I have lived for twelve years, beside the bones of my seventeen departed brethren." And he closes his letter thus :—"Lastly, O father, pray for us, even as we, though small and of little account, pray for you; and do not look upon us as strangers; for whether Gauls, Britons, or Irish, or of whatever nation, we are members of one Body. Let us rejoice in the faith and knowledge of the Son of God, and hasten to attain unto a perfect man, unto the measure of the stature of the fulness of Christ, so that we may each be a blessing to the other, and care and pray for each other."

About the same time, and on similar subjects, he wrote to Pope Gregory the Great, and afterwards to Pope Boniface IV.; not that he for a moment recognized their authority; his letters are pervaded by that spirit of independence which characterized the British Church; but he could not shut his eyes to the fact that the Popes already exercised a vast amount of power and influence in the Frankish Church, and he called upon them to use their power in the Name and for the honour of Christ.

Not many years after this another attack was made upon Columban; but this time it came from a totally different quarter, and was of a totally different kind. His monasteries were situated in the territory of Thierri II., king of Burgundy, whose brother, Theodebert, ruled the neighbouring kingdom of Austrasia. The name and character of Columban had already given him some influence over the mind of the voluptuous Thierri, when a change was made by the sudden arrival of the infamous Brunehaut, grandmother of Thierri, flying from the court of Theodebert at Metz, where her pride and cruelty had roused the nobles of Austrasia against her. Her violent and unscrupulous spirit immediately asserted its ascendency over Thierri, whom she ruled through his vices, and the king plunged more deeply than ever into voluptuous excess. His wife, daughter of the king of the Visigoths, persecuted and tormented by the arts of Brunehaut, fled to her father's court. In some moment of remorse Thierri was induced to visit Columban in his retirement, and the man of God sternly and fearlessly rebuked him for his adulteries and other crimes. The king listened with awe and promised to amend. Brunehaut, more frantic with rage than ever, resolved upon the destruction of one who seemed likely to thwart all her schemes of ambition. At last Columban was arrested and carried to Besançon. But his guards, knowing who their prisoner was, performed their duty purposely with such negligence that they allowed him to escape and return to Luxeuil. Again he was seized and carried off amid the lamentations of his faithful followers. Two or three Irish monks were allowed to accompany him, and they were hurried to Nantes to be embarked in a vessel and sent back to Ireland. But in every city there were some few, at all events, whose sympathy was roused by the mention of his name. While he and his companions were in the cell at Nantes a beggar came before it, and Columban ordered the last measure of meal in their possession to be given to the hungry man. The next two days he himself had nothing to satisfy his hunger, but he continued joyful in faith and hope, when suddenly a knock was heard at the door. The servant of a pious female in the city had come with a supply of corn and wine.

The vessel in which he was embarked was cast by a storm on the coast of the kingdom of Neustria, a territory which extended from the Meuse to the ocean. A message came from Theodebert of Austrasia, offering an asylum and a residence in his dominions. But Columban declined the invitation, and he and his little party made their way to Mentz and embarked upon the Rhine. For many days they worked up the stream, till at last they reached the mouth of the Limmat, and they then followed that river till they arrived at the Lake of Zurich. They then crossed country to Zug, where they made their first halt. They were now in the land of the Suevi, heathen and barbarians, and to them they preached the Gospel. Before long, however, they were compelled to fly. They retraced their steps to the Lake of Zurich, and after crossing it they made their way to Arbon, on the Lake of Constance. This was an old Roman fortified place on an eminence overlooking the lake. Here they found remains of old civilization and a Christian priest named Willimar. He told them of a spot where they might hope to find a permanent resting-place, an old Roman town at the end of the lake, deserted and ruined, the site of what is now Bregenz. Here they remained between two and three years, but at the end of this time Cunzo, a neighbouring chieftain, instigated not improbably by Brunehaut and Thierri, roused a persecution against them, and Columban determined to retire. He sought and found a retreat in Lombardy, where he was favourably received by the king.

Advancing years had put an end to his labours among the wild and barbarous heathen, but he had still strength to bring a blessing to the distracted Church of North Italy. His efforts to promote unity and peace, and to edify Christians by his writings, were attended with no little success. At last, by the favour of the king, he was able to establish on the northern slopes of the Apennines, far up the river Trebia, the monastery of Bobbio, famous for its library and its learning in later times; and here, in his seventy-second year, he passed away from this world. He had scattered the seed of the Word in the East of France, in Switzerland, and in the North of Italy, and he had trained a large band of scholars to follow his bright example.

ST. GALL AND THE DISCIPLES OF COLUMBAN.

THE most distinguished of the chosen twelve who were Columban's companions when he left Ireland on his missionary enterprise was Gallus, or Gall. He was descended from a respectable Irish family, and in very early youth he was entrusted by his parents to Columban to be educated for the service of the kingdom of God. This was when Columban was an inmate of the monastery of Bangor. The Irish monasteries were, as we have seen, remarkable for the zeal and diligence with which the Scriptures were studied in them, and Columban was among the most assiduous students in the monastery of Bangor. He had long and deeply studied the Scriptures himself, and his familiarity with them is shown by every page of his writings; and he laboured unceasingly to attract his pupils towards the same sacred pursuit. He possessed in an unusual degree the power of applying the words of Scripture to the varying circumstances of the moment, to speak with simplicity and at the same time with earnestness, and to make his hearers feel that the questions of their hearts and their inmost longings were answered by the Word of God. Hence it is no wonder that he exerted a very powerful influence in this direction over those who were entrusted to his charge. His pupils felt that they were not merely being taught the words of a book, but that they were learning how to live. Among those who felt this charm, and who yielded to it most, was Gallus; and when the day came for Columban to leave his native land for Christ's sake, the Irish love of travel and adventure, personal affection for a master to whom he owed so much, as well as the constraining sense of a high calling, combined to make it impossible for Gallus to remain behind. He seems to have been Columban's favourite pupil. When they were travelling towards Anegratis, and afterwards, when they went on short expeditions to preach the Gospel to the heathen round them, if in any spot they happened to meet with well-disposed persons who gave them a hospitable reception, they laid their baggage down upon the ground to rest for a little while, and read the Scriptures. On these occasions it was Gallus who was called upon to be the reader, Gallus who was bidden to repeat any words of wisdom which he could remember to have heard or read in explanation of the passage upon which he had opened. We hear, however, very little of Gallus until after Columban's banishment from Burgundy and after his arrival at Arbon on the Lake of Constance. There their sudden presence cheered the lonely labours of Willimar, who was struggling, amid all discouragement and hardship, to bear his witness for Christ among the heathen; and in Willimar Gallus found a friend who was destined to be afterwards a source of strength and blessing to himself. By Willimar's advice they went up the lake to the ancient ruins of Bregenz; and here Gallus begins to be a prominent character in the group, and even sometimes to take an apparent lead. His age is not known. Perhaps he was still in early youth when he left his native land, and the twenty-five years which had passed since then had, on the one hand, brought him to the full prime and strength of manhood, and, on the other, so far advanced his master in age that he was beginning to feel his strength abating and his vigour decaying, and he was willing, in all labours which required activity and bodily energy, to yield precedence to a pupil whom he had found to be so likeminded with himself.

Another cause which tended to make Gallus increasingly prominent in the district which they were now endeavouring to evangelize was his power of acquiring foreign languages. There were now in the country of the Alemanni, a German people who had taken permanent possession of that region, and whose descendants in the north-east of Switzerland still speak their original German tongue, while French is the language of the south-west. During his long residence in the Frankish kingdom, and his frequent missionary journeys from Anegratis and Luxeuil, Gallus had made good use of his opportunities of learning to speak the German language. So that in this respect he was completely at home round the Lake of Constance, and, if Columban continued to be the leader, Gallus was the chief speaker of the party.

Among the ruins of the ancient castle of Bregenz they found an old dilapidated shrine. It was itself in ruins, but there were signs of recent or present use, for it contained three statues of pagan deities in gilded brass. They determined to consecrate this shrine for Christian worship, and they constructed their cells close to it. As their purpose became known great numbers of people flocked together to witness the ceremony and see the

ST. GALL AND THE DISCIPLES OF COLUMBAN. 61

manner in which the strangers served their God. It was an opportunity not to be passed by, and Gallus sought permission from Columban to preach the Gospel to the people. The crowd listened attentively while he delivered to them the message of the kingdom of God, and by degrees his words stirred them to a consciousness of spiritual things and of a Spirit pleading with their spirits. It is at such a moment that men feel the vanity and nothingness of outward things, and the helplessness of gods of gold and silver and wood and stone. While the minds of his hearers were still full of the thoughts which his words had stirred, and while the impression upon their hearts was still vivid, Gallus seized the occasion to establish for ever by an outward sign the authority of the Truth which he proclaimed. While yet speaking he boldly made his way to the three statues which were still the objects of pagan adoration, and before the very eyes of the astonished multitude he dashed them in pieces one after the other with rapid strokes and hurled them into the lake. The crowd looked on in silence, some in awe, some in anger, but none ventured to interfere, and the impression of the blow which he struck that day did not soon pass away.

For a long time no one molested the little party of Christian men. They immediately began their usual occupation of tilling the earth and subduing it, and marking it out for God. They turned the dilapidated shrine into a Christian church. They reclaimed a portion of land and turned it into a garden; they planted fruit-trees; and the pagans watched and admired the first beginnings of civilized life. Soon Gallus began to weave nets and to catch the fish which abounded in the lake and were to furnish them with a large proportion of their subsistence. It was now and then only, and by good fortune rather than any skill of their own, that the barbarous tribes had been able to avail themselves of this obvious means of support. Their gratitude was great when Gallus taught them how to do as he did himself and, meanwhile, made presents to them of the fish which he caught. In this way he established terms of amity between the missionary band and the people who surrounded them, and prepared the way for exerting a higher and holier influence.

After three years, however, the malignity of Brunehaut and Thierri pursued them, as we have seen, even into this retreat, and the persecutions of Cunzo compelled them to break up their little establishment. Gallus was at this time disabled by a serious illness, which made it impossible for him to accompany Columban on his journey across the mountains into Italy. They parted in anxiety and sorrow, and never met on earth again, and Gallus was left alone in this wild and inhospitable region. He called to mind the kindness of Willimar three years before. Was Willimar still living? Was he still at Arbon? Had he himself strength to reach the place? Then he would at all events enjoy once again the solace of human sympathy and friendship. He managed to embark in his little boat, and took his fishing-nets with him, and set out alone to float down the lake to Arbon. His voyage was successful, and he met at Arbon with the warm reception upon which he had confidently counted. Willimar gave the sick man in charge to two of his clergy, and by their constant and loving care he was restored to health.

A legend relating to Gallus is mentioned by Dean Milman in his "History of Latin Christianity," and illustrates in a picturesque and striking manner the feeling which existed in men's minds that such persons were attended by a special providence and carried with them a heavenly influence. While Gallus, one silent night, was fishing in the Lake of

Constance, he heard a voice which appeared to come from one of the highest peaks around him. It was the Spirit of the Mountains calling to the Spirit of the Waters in the depth of the lake. Then came a reply, " I am here." And the voice cried, " Arise, and help me against these strangers who have driven me from my temple; let us cast them out of the land." And again an answer came, " One of them is at this moment busy in my waters, but I cannot even break his nets. I am rebuked by the prevailing Name in which he is perpetually praying." This is one of those myths which enclose a kernel of truth within a shell of invention. Gallus was surrounded by the powers of darkness, but none of them could by any means hurt him, because of the Name which is above every name.

Gallus had resorted to Willimar in his extremity, but he had no intention of making his permanent abode at Arbon. His desire was to find some spot which he might fix upon for a hermitage, and where he might establish a new centre of light and blessing for the heathen people round. But he was wholly unacquainted with the neighbourhood. As soon, therefore, as he had recovered his strength, he begged Willimar for his counsel and for a guide.

In the division of labour at Arbon it had fallen to the lot of the deacon Hillibald to provide such supplies of food for the community as could be obtained by hunting and fishing. This occupation had, many times over, led him through all parts of the surrounding country, and he was better acquainted than any one else with the tracks of the forest. To this man Willimar referred Gallus for the knowledge which he sought. All he asked was a place where he could build himself a cell, and where he was sure of a supply of water; for all things else he depended upon his own exertions and the help of God. Hillibald gave him a fearful description of the dangers to which he would be exposed, the wild beasts, wolves, bears, boars, with which the forest abounded. But Gallus only answered, " If God be for us, who can be against us? All things work together for good to them that love Him. He saved Daniel from the lions' den, and He will deliver me from the wild beasts which are in this forest." Then the deacon answered, " Put some bread and a little net into your knapsack; to-morrow I will take you into the forest. God has brought you here from a distant land; He will send His angel with us, as He sent him with Tobias, and show you such a place as you are desiring according to His will." Gallus spent that day in prayer and fasting, and, after further prayer, he started next morning on his perilous way, with the deacon for his companion. Upwards they went from the shore of the lake, till the waters were hidden as they climbed through the forest. For many a weary hour, from early morning till two or three o'clock in the afternoon, they travelled on; and then Hillibald said, "Let us try to catch some fish in the stream, and eat some bread, that we may have strength for the rest of the way." But Gallus answered, "My son, do what is necessary for yourself: I will taste nothing till God has pointed out to me the place of my rest." Then said the deacon, "If that be so, we will share the labour together, and afterwards we will share the joy." So they went on till set of sun. Then they came to a place where the river Steinach, precipitating itself from the mountain's side, had hollowed out a basin in the rock, and they could see the fish, in great numbers, swimming in the stream. They caught several in the net. Hillibald struck fire with a flint, broiled the fish, took bread out of their knapsack, and prepared for supper. But before they sat down to eat Gallus went apart a little distance to pray. As he went his foot caught in a thornbush, and he fell. The deacon ran to his assistance, but he motioned him away, saying, "God has shown me the place of my rest; here will I abide as long as I live." He immediately consecrated the place by prayer, and when he rose from his knees he made a cross of a hazel rod and planted it in the earth to mark the spot.

Hillibald returned to Arbon, and left Gallus by himself once more. At first there was but a single cell, his own, from which, as a centre, he issued forth to spread the Word of life; but, by degrees, first one and then another was attracted to him, and came to him to be taught; the cells began to multiply, the forest to be cleared, the land to be cultivated, and at last a monastery arose, which afterwards became celebrated. It was called by the name of St. Gall, and gave the same to the canton in which it stood.

Gallus had now obtained the object of his longing desire. He was a centre from which temporal and spiritual blessings were scattered far and wide. He laboured in the education of the young, and in the training of monks and clergy, who might in turn become a blessing to the world, and follow in his steps as he had himself followed in those of his master Columban. After this work had been going on some time, and his name had become widely known, he used sometimes to receive presents from wealthy persons, to be used for the benefit of his monastery or spent as he pleased. On such occasions he assembled the poor and needy of the neighbourhood in crowds and distributed to them what he had received. Once, at such at time, one of his scholars said to him, " My father, I have a costly silver vessel, beautifully enchased; if you approve, I will not give it away, but keep it to be used at the Holy Supper." But Gallus answered, " My son, think of Peter's words, ' Silver and gold have I none.' Follow his example; hasten and dispose of it for the good of the poor. My master Columban used to distribute the holy elements in a vessel of brass."

After some years had passed in this way, Gallus received an invitation pressing him to accept the bishopric of Costnitz, which was then vacant. But he felt that he was in his place where he was, and that he would not be justified in forsaking his post. But he recommended for the office the deacon John, a native of the country, who had been trained under his own direction. John was elected, and a large concourse of people of every rank in life came together to witness his consecration. The sermon which Gallus delivered on this occasion is still preserved. He entered the pulpit in company with John, who interpreted in the dialect of the country what Gallus delivered in Latin.

After this Gallus continued to labour for many years for the salvation of the Swiss and Suabian populations dwelling round his monastery. At last, feeling his death approaching, he begged his old friend, the priest Willimar, to meet him at the Castle of Arbon. Feeble as he was he roused himself to preach to the assembled people. But this was his last effort. Sickness made his return impossible, and he died at Arbon in 640.

The life of Gallus is but a specimen of the manner in which the pupils of Columban worked on in his spirit. The number of these Irish monks who passed over to France from their native country was very great, and the stream continued through the seventh century. But not only was the example set by Columban, not only did nearly all those who followed him adopt his rule, but his direct spiritual descendants were extremely numerous. The frontier line between the Church and the heathen was dotted over by strongholds of his erection or that of his disciples. They were winning back in the name of Christ districts which Roman civilization had lost to advancing barbarism. In this way there issued from the British Church almost a race of saints, the founders of some of the most important establishments within or on the borders of the old Roman territory, such as were Magnoald of Fussen, on the Lech, Attalus of Bobbio, Romaric of Remiremont, St. Omer, St. Bertin, St. Amand, the Apostles of Flanders, St. Wandrille, the founder of Fontenelle in Normandy, and many others.

Gradually the great establishments founded on the rule of St. Columban dropped the few peculiarities of discipline which distinguished them, and nothing but their dress marked them as distinct from the other monasteries of the West.

ST. BONIFACE.

COLUMBAN and his disciples, although they greatly extended the knowledge of the Gospel along the frontier line of the old Roman Empire, scarcely at any point passed permanently beyond its limits. They established a chain of outposts along the verge of Christendom, and in districts which had reverted to barbarism; and they gradually encircled themselves with an enlarging belt of cultivation and of Christian light, but so far as the outer world of heathendom was concerned they were only thus slowly and indirectly aggressive. They laid a foundation and established a basis for the future operations of others. They laboured, but others were to enter into their labours, and carry the light of the kingdom into the very midst of the habitations of darkness. But another generation had to pass before this was done, and when the time came it was from the British Isles once more that the messengers of the Cross went forth;' from them again the light shined. But meanwhile a great change had taken place in the British Isles themselves.

When Columban, on his way from Ireland to France, had passed within sight of the shores of England, he looked upon them with horror, for the old British Church, from whence Patrick had gone to win Ireland for Christ, had been driven into mountainous Wales and far-away Cornwall and Cumberland and Scotland, and the Saxon conquerors who filled the land were heathens, and the land was dark with superstition and pagan idolatry. But times had changed. Gregory, Bishop of Rome, had sent Augustine to England, and there was an Archbishop of Canterbury at last, and the standard of Christ was set up finally and firmly in the island, and was soon to cover the whole of it.

But Ireland had already become the Isle of Saints, and was setting England an example in works of peace and holiness. Many a young Englishman went over to Ireland in the last times of the seventh century, that he might be able to lead a silent and spiritual life among the monks, and gather sacred and other knowledge from their stores, far away from the tumult and temptations of Anglo-Saxon England. Such persons always received a hearty welcome. The Irish were always ready to entertain strangers, remembering, perhaps, that their own wandering spirit might make them strangers to-morrow in some foreign land. Among these guests from England was one whose name was Egbert. While he was living in Ireland he fell sick, and his sickness seemed likely to end in death, and he vowed a vow that if it pleased God to spare his life this time, he would never return to his native land, but would spend all his days serving God in some foreign country. He recovered, and remembering his vow he cast about whither he should go. At last, with several companions, he determined to go to the German tribes and preach the Gospel to them. When they were on the point of embarking, he was detained behind, and he himself laboured among the Scots and Picts, but his companions carried the first resolution into effect, so that it was Egbert who gave the first impulse to the work which left its mark upon Germany for ever. One of the band was Wigbert. For two years he struggled in hope and fear among the Frieslanders, but the fierceness of the people and their King Radbod was so great that he was forced after that time to return to his native land; and he seemed to have accomplished nothing. Then went Wilbrord. He had come from England when he was twenty, full of good resolutions, and looking forward into an unknown future of study and self-improvement. Now he was thirty-two, and he began to feel that none of us liveth to himself and none of us dieth to himself, and it was time that he too should be a blessing to the world and labour outwardly for Christ. Were not the Saxons from whom his own forefathers sprang still heathen? and could not something be done to save even those fierce Frieslanders, who, heathen though they were, were making themselves a name? And was not all Germany in the background? Where was there a field of labour so great, and where were the labourers so few? And now, too, Pepin, Mayor of the Palace of the Franks, had overcome the Frieslanders in battle, and some of them were dependent on the Frankish Empire; so there was a better opening than ever there had been before.

But how should he set to work? Those were evil times. God's order and peace were slowly and hardly making their way against the confusion and disorder of the world. Kings were not the nursing fathers of the Church, nor were queens her nursing mothers. Often they were her bitterest enemies, and she looked about for some one to lean upon. Over and over again, when the light of the Gospel was flickering and going out, in one land or another, the Bishop of Rome had kept it alight, and trimmed the flame. Over and over again, when iniquity and wrong seemed triumphant, the Bishop of Rome had made the oppressor tremble with the word that the Judge of all the earth would see right done. Every day men were more and more looking to Rome for help and strength against violence and misrule. We know what this came to afterwards. Violence and misrule set up their throne in Rome itself, and the Bishop of Rome, who had been such a blessing in helping men to remember their Father in heaven, called himself their father instead, and did not hold forth the word of light, but covered it. Woe to him who hides from the children's eyes the face of their Father, and when they are starving and ask for the bread of their home, gives them a stone in its place! But these things were not so as yet. Men did not know what was coming in after times. They used the help that God offered them, and trusted the future to Him. So Wilbrord went on his journey to Rome, and told all his heart to Pope Sergius, and came back full of hope and formally commissioned to his work. Why should he have done this? Why should he have thought he needed that commission? We must not be in haste to blame him. Remember that it was Pope Gregory who sent Augustine to preach the Gospel in England. If it had not been for Pope Gregory, Wilbrord himself would have been a heathen still. And only twenty-four years ago Pope Vitalian had sent Archbishop Theodore to Canterbury, and Wilbrord knew what a deep debt of gratitude the English Church owed the Pope for that. It was no wonder that he wished to have the Pope's blessing before he started. But it was a pity, for it set an example which others followed, and much harm came of it.

Wilbrord was not long in coming back from Rome, and Pepin was very ready to help him when he did. In the part of Friesland which Pepin had conquered there was an old Roman town, Trajectum; he wished to make this the metropolis of the district, and the mother-Church of that country. So Wilbrord was consecrated Archbishop of Trajectum, as Augustine was of Canterbury. We all know the place now under the name of Utrecht. Here Wilbrord lived and laboured for many a year. Fierce Radbod still lived, and all efforts were unavailing to touch his heart. But Wilbrord once took a circuit, and got beyond the king's dominions as far as Denmark. Here he had a little success, for he persuaded thirty of the native lads to join him and be instructed by him as he travelled. After a time he was forced to take ship upon the German Ocean towards England. But they came in sight of a certain island, and when they landed they found that it was Fosite's land, consecrated to the German deity Fosite. It still bears a name which keeps up the memory of its consecration, Heligoland, Holy Island. By this time the thirty lads were prepared for baptism, and Wilbrord found a fountain and was administering the holy rite. But suddenly they were interrupted by wild shouts; numbers of the natives were crowding round them in fury and threatening them with instant death. The fountain, it seemed, was consecrated to Fosite, and none might live who dared to touch it. One of the missionaries, selected by lot, was sacrificed to the idol; the rest King Radbod, with unusual self-restraint, sent back to the kingdom of the Franks. Wilbrord went back to Utrecht, and

78 CHRISTIAN MISSIONS BEFORE THE REFORMATION.

laboured among Pepin's subjects, and kept a watchful eye open, hoping against hope for the Frieslanders beyond the border. In 719 Radbod was called to his account, and the doors were opened for the messengers of the Cross. The next twenty years were a bright time for Wilbrord, and repaid him well for all the suffering and anxiety of the past. In 739 he entered into his rest, old and full of years.

Wilbrord was, as yet, by far the most conspicuous of the English missionaries, but besides him a great number of others, whose names are scarcely known, were making separate and scattered efforts, all along the old Roman frontier, to carry the Gospel into Germany; but it was only like a line of sparks of fire, casting in quick succession a beam or two of light into the darkness, and then being sadly too often themselves extinguished. It was much better than nothing, no doubt, but these little beams could scarcely even make a twilight, so far apart were they and so weak. If high noon was ever to come it would be in some other way. Some strong wise man must arise, who would be able to direct the whole and work upon a settled plan and system, so that the sparks, which were being extinguished separately in the cold and dark, should run together and form one grand flame. Who was to be the man? He must be one of great zeal and strong will, must know how to command and yet how to yield, strong and firm yet pliant and considerate, ready to do and to dare, not easily dreaming of lions in the path, though lions there were sure enough which might quell the courage of any man who was not filled with some secret life and strength. There was a man who already felt himself called to this work, and who did it at last. In later ages men called him "Apostle of Germany," and assuredly he was an Apostle "sent" by God to carry light and life to the tribes of Germany sitting in darkness and death. But a man can only pass on to others what he has himself, and we have reached a time now in the eighth century when the light of truth was seldom to be had pure, the clear white ray of heaven was mixed with tints of other colours reflected from the things of earth. The next great English Missionary brought a very precious gift, but he did not give it quite undefiled.

Winfrid was born at Crediton in Devonshire, in 680, so that he was a boy of twelve when Wilbrord went to Rome before beginning his work at Utrecht. His father was a man of some wealth and consideration, who could have done much to push him forward in the world, and who accordingly destined him for some post of secular distinction. It was an old and excellent custom in the Church of England for the clergy to visit frequently the more conspicuous houses of the laity, where families were large and servants many, and, when the household was collected together, to give instruction in the Scriptures, the life of our blessed Lord, and the chief points of the Creed. When the clergyman spoke from the heart, the children loved to listen, and many instances are on record of impressions of religion made in this way upon the heart of a child and never afterwards effaced. Winfrid was one of these instances. His heart was inflamed by what he heard from time to time, and the desire which he felt to devote himself to a religious life became settled by degrees into a fixed resolution. When he declared his purpose, his father was miserably disappointed, and used every means to turn his son's attention to other things. But all his efforts seemed only to fix more firmly the inclination which he was labouring to destroy, and at last when his own spirit was broken by a heavy reverse of fortune, he allowed his son to have his way. Winfrid lost no time in obtaining admission to the monastery at Exeter, and in commencing his direct preparation for a clerical life.

It was almost a custom for a youth, on entering a monastery with the intention of permanently devoting himself to the religious life, to drop the name by which he had been hitherto known, and to assume another. Winfrid would be willing enough to comply with this custom. He was not sorry to exhibit to his family this outward sign of his unchangeable resolve. Old things had passed away, all things were to become new. It was perhaps at this time that he assumed the name by which he became afterwards known in history. He had been Winfrid, the "Friend of Peace," he was now for evermore to be Boniface, the Active Doer of Good.

But he had not been long at Exeter before he left it to complete his training at Nhutscelle. If, as there is some reason to believe, this was the abbey afterwards called Netley, then was—

"Tree-girt Netley, from the inland tide
Seen fair, as summer vessels downward glide"—

and no doubt the sight of the vessels which, even in those early days, were sometimes to be seen sailing down Southampton Water, helped to keep alive in him his strong desire to preach the Gospel in foreign lands. But many years were to pass before his time should come. Meanwhile he was busy about matters which lay closer to his hand than the heathen abroad. He studied hard to gain a wide and deep knowledge of the Holy Scriptures, and so to lay in a store from which he might afterwards draw in times of need. And his heart and mind were not confined within the walls of his cell. He early distinguished himself by prudence and skill in the management of affairs; when any delicate and difficult business had to be done for the convent, he was usually the doer of it. Once there was danger of a collision between the Clergy of Wessex and Berthwald, Archbishop of Canterbury. They had held a synod before his arrival and without waiting for his leave. They fixed upon the young and persuasive monk of Nhutscelle for the delicate task of going as their deputy to Berthwald to explain what they had done and soothe the Primate's wrath. He went, and so effectually accomplished his task that he won the personal affection of Berthwald, and many times in his later letters he speaks of the help which the Archbishop's patronage had afforded to him. He was learning human nature and how to manage men.

He was now about thirty years old, and he was ordained priest. Then soon after there came upon him that passion for foreign travel, and that loftier impulse to devote himself to the spread of the kingdom of God, which so many of his countrymen had already felt. He knew what Wilbrord was doing at Utrecht, and it became the longing of his heart to join him. Loath to lose him, but wholly unable to bend him from his purpose, the Abbot of Nhutscelle gave a reluctant consent, and Boniface sailed from London for Friesland. When he landed, war was raging between Charles Martel and fierce King Radbod, and the Franks just then were driven back, and the persecution of the Christians in Friesland was at its hottest. Everywhere in the land the churches were destroyed, the heathen temples rebuilt. Wilbrord would not forsake his post, but he persuaded Boniface to leave him, and return for the present to his convent. He reached Nhutscelle just in time to be present at Abbot Winbert's funeral. Would Boniface be the new Abbot in his place? The monks of his cloister were very anxious that he should, and they pressed it upon him again and again. It was a good work which they were asking him to do; but the fear of Christ, as he calls it, was strong upon him and would not let him rest. He looked upon himself as under a debt *to the heathen,* which at all costs he must pay for Christ's sake. Woe was unto him if he remained at home and preached not the Gospel in heathen lands! In this way God marks men out for different spheres of work. A strong inward impulse, coupled with the possession of necessary qualifications for a particular work, is often a sign from heaven of what the Captain of the host would have a man do.

So Boniface would not be Abbot, but prepared at once to start once more for heathen lands. And now he did what he had not done when he started for the first time, and one cannot help wishing he had never done at all. Why should he go to Rome and ask the Pope's authority for what he was going to do? Wilbrord had gone, and Pope Sergius had blessed him in his work, and the Popes were ready enough to put a meaning into such visits which the visitors themselves never intended. But unhappily Boniface himself intended a great deal. He had more than half a belief that, unless the Pope commissioned him, he would have no business to preach Christ to the Germans. "How shall they preach," he remembered it was said, "except they be sent?" And he never reflected that he himself was already sent, and inwardly called to this particular work, and outwardly ordained and commissioned by the bishops of his own Church.

What more could he want? But men were beginning now to look upon the Pope as the source of all authority in Christendom, and in the English Church, fresh from its conversion by Roman Augustine, the feeling was especially strong. In this way good and earnest men were unconsciously and by degrees building up a power which in their own time was usually harmless and often full of blessing, but which in after times was to become at last a thing from which they would have shrunk with horror.

Boniface must needs go to Rome to ask leave of Gregory II. to obey the call which he had received already. He sailed this time, some say (but why I know not), from Bonchurch in the Isle of Wight, a place which may likely enough have been named after him when his name became great. He crossed the sea to Normandy, not alone but one of a multitude of pilgrims, and he journeyed slowly through France, stopping at all the more famous churches to pay his adorations there. At last he reached the Alps and crossed them, no slight labour and peril in those days, and he came down the mountains into lovely and beautiful but wild and savage Lombardy—lovely and beautiful as God meant it to be, wild and savage as man had made it. Disorder and anarchy were triumphant there, rapine and bloodshed filled the land, fierce bands of robbers were the terror of such as were compelled to pass that way. But Boniface escaped these dangers, and found himself at last on his knees in the church of St. Peter at Rome. His friend, Daniel, Bishop of Winchester, had given him letters of recommendation to the Pope, so that he received a kind and courteous welcome. Pope Gregory II. entered heartily into all his views and sanctioned his passionate desire to carry the message of peace to the savage tribes of Germany. It was now late in the autumn of 718. He remained at Rome through the winter, finally preparing himself for the work before him; and early in May of the next year he started for East Franconia. Here, in the country round Bamberg and Nuremberg, the scattered efforts of individual missionaries had had no inconsiderable effect, and the Gospel was more or less known among the people. In Thuringia the same was partially the case; but from Lower Hesse eastward towards Saxony heathenism was still supreme; and even in Thuringia the little progress which had been made was already being gradually lost. He settled himself for a time in Thuringia, but he seemed to accomplish nothing. What appeared to be gained one day was lost the next. Musing over the causes of his ill-success he became convinced that without powerful assistance from without for the protection of himself and his converts, and for the support of the mission, no firm and lasting impression would be made. The Pope had given him letters of recommendation to all the Bishops and to all orders of Christians in the Church of the Franks, and this alone secured to him one great advantage which had not been possessed by Columban. Where coldness and even ill-will had been shown to the one, the other found sympathy and sometimes co-operation. But this was not all he wanted. He had come to the conclusion that the outward and material aid of the secular power was absolutely necessary to protect his churches and convents from the pagans, who were always on the watch for an opportunity to destroy them; to secure the lives of the monks and nuns whom he had sent for from England to preach to the pagan idolaters and to educate those who were willing to be taught; to procure the necessary means of subsistence, for it was only here and there that they were allowed to cultivate the ground in peace, and so provide for themselves. Besides these there was yet another point to which Boniface attached the greatest possible importance, and in which he needed the support of the secular power. When the light of the Gospel had found its way into any district, and the people had begun willingly to listen to the preaching of the missionary, it often happened that the effect of his words was destroyed, and the impression weakened if not effaced, by the visible presence of some old object of idolatry, to which the people had been accustomed for generations to pay religious worship. If these things could be destroyed in each place where their influence over the minds of the people was for a moment weakened by the preaching of the Cross, it would be less easy to entangle them once more in their former superstition.

But in all this he felt the need of external help, and there was only one source from whence such help could come. Charles Martel, or rather simple Charles, for he had not yet won his proud title by "*hammering*" Abderrahman and his Saracens out of Christendom; Charles Martel, Mayor of the Palace of the Franks, had all the royal power though he never took the name of king, and was the most powerful ruler in Western Europe. Boniface must make up his mind to use a letter of recommendation which Gregory had given him to this potentate, but which he seems to have reserved as yet, perhaps in the hope that he might conquer by spiritual arms alone. Men might not listen more humbly to a *protégé* of Charles, but at all events they would be more afraid to touch him to his harm.

To the court of Charles therefore he now went and presented Gregory's letter. It was found to contain an urgent request that Charles would assist the missionary by every means in his power in the pious and Christian work of reclaiming the heathen "from the condition of brute beasts." Charles was very ready to do as he was requested. He provided Boniface with letters of safety, declaring him under the protection of the Franks; any one who allowed him to be molested or ill-treated in his work must expect vengeance and speedy retribution. These were no mere words. When Charles Martel spoke, men generally understood that he meant what he said, and there was no doubt of his power to enforce his will. In a letter which Boniface wrote long after to his friend Daniel, of Winchester, he says, " Without the mighty protection of the Prince of the Franks, I could neither rule the people, nor defend the priests, the monks, and the handmaids of God, nor put down pagan and idolatrous rites in Germany."

His thoughts by day and dreams by night were now full of the hope and cheer with which the countenance of Charles inspired him. He had a dream in which he seemed to see a whole region covered with fields of corn stretching far and wide to all quarters under heaven, and ready for the reaping; and One came to him and gave him a sickle that he might go forth and reap the rich and abundant harvest. Then came tidings which seemed to show that it was not all a dream. Messengers from Utrecht said that Radbod was dead. The door was wide open which had before been so fast closed against himself; Wilbrord would be speeding through it to win the Frieslanders for Christ; Boniface must fly to his help; the harvest was begun. Quick as oars and sails could speed him he made his way down the Rhine to Utrecht, and found Wilbrord, as he expected, with a head full of plans of action, and a heart full of joy and hope. Three long years he stayed with Wilbrord, and the wisdom and experience of the one, and the zeal and energy of the other, accomplished much in widening the boundaries of the Church and deepening her hold upon the people of the land. But Wilbrord was growing old, and felt his strength already failing. It could not be very long before he would be called away. How could he better provide for the Church he loved so well than by securing for it the services of one so full of zeal and wisdom as Boniface, now in the prime of life and vigour? Boniface must surely stay on, and be bishop, his coadjutor now, his successor afterwards. But Boniface would not listen to argument or entreaty. At last he could bear it no longer. He declared that he had a special mission to preach the Gospel in Germany proper; he had already delayed too long in Friesland; he dared no longer delay the duties which more particularly belonged to himself.

So Wilbrord and Boniface parted again for the second time and the last, and Boniface betook himself finally to his portion of the great harvest field. In Thuringia, then ceaselessly harried by the bordering Saxons, and in wholly heathen Hesse, he worked with much better success than before, and baptized many, and founded the monastery of Amæneburg.

As we have seen so much of the store which he set by external help, and his readiness to seek and welcome the assistance of the powers of the world in the battle which he was fighting for Christ, it would be treating him hardly if we did not look for a moment upon the other side of the matter. He was leading an inward life which was intensely real, and he was deeply and thoroughly aware that, though Paul may plant and Apollos water, it is God alone Who can give the increase. In a letter to some English Christian women he says, " I beseech you to pray fervently to the Lord, as, indeed, I believe that you already do, that we may be redeemed from wicked and mischievous men, for all men have not faith; and be assured that we praise God, though the sufferings of our heart are many. May the Lord our God, Who is the refuge of the poor and the hope of the humble, deliver us from the temptations of this evil world, that the glorious Gospel of Christ may be glorified, that the grace of the Lord shown to me may not be in vain. Let me not die without having brought forth fruit for the Gospel; let me not depart without leaving sons and daughters behind; so that when the Lord comes I may not be found to have hidden my talent, and receive punishment rather than reward from Him that sent me." To a young man in England he gave this counsel:—"Throw aside everything that hinders you, and direct your whole study to the Holy Scripture, and there seek that Divine wisdom which is more precious than gold; for what is it more seemly in youth to strive after, or what can age possess more precious, than the knowledge of the Holy Scriptures, which will guide our souls safely through the tempest to the shores of the heavenly Paradise, to the eternal joys of angels?" Among the friends in England who remembered and loved him there was one, the Abbess Eadburga, who used from time to time to send him clothes and books, the latter being now more easily met with in England than anywhere else. Once, when she had sent him a Bible, he wrote in reply, "that she had consoled him in his banishment with spiritual light: for whoever is obliged to visit the dark corners of the German people falls into the jaws of death, unless he has the Word of God as a lantern to his feet and a light unto his path." At another time he called to mind a manuscript of the Prophets which, he remembered, used to belong to his departed abbot and teacher, Wimbert, at Nhutscelle, and which was written in very plain and distinct characters. He wrote to his friend Daniel of Winchester, begging him, if possible, to procure this manuscript and send it to him. "If God incline you to grant this request, you can render no greater comfort to my old age; for in this country I cannot obtain such a manuscript of the Prophets as I wish for, and now that my eyes are weak I cannot distinguish small and closely written characters and abbreviations." In the same way he begged the Abbess Eadburga to send him a copy of the Epistles of St. Peter, written in gilt letters. But these requests were made in later years, when the prime of his life was passed. He is now in the vigour of his manhood, battling in Thuringia and heathen Hesse.

He kept up as brisk communication as he could, both with Daniel and with Pope Gregory II. When he wrote to the latter, telling of the success which attended his efforts and of the foundation of Amæneburg, he was summoned by the Pope to visit Rome once more. It was time, so Gregory thought, that new and higher powers should be given him, to carry on with still greater effect the work which he had so well begun. After a more detailed account of his labours, and after a solemn confession of his faith, he was consecrated Bishop of the Church in Germany. No special diocese was for the present assigned to him; his labours were to be confined to no one place, but he was to travel round among the tribes, and to spend the most of his time wherever necessity might require. In this manner distinct authority was given to him to direct according to his wisdom the work which was being done in Germany. The separate efforts of individual missionaries should cease to be isolated and desultory; all were to be combined into one army of the Cross, acting upon a regular system and directed by one head.

This was a very great advantage, and, considering the spirit of the times and the circumstances of the particular case, it may be questioned whether without this close organization, and without this support from the Bishop of Rome, the Christian Church could have been securely planted in Germany until centuries of delay had passed. But a heavy price had to be paid. First of all, Boniface was placed in greater or less antagonism to many of the missionaries already at work, and who breathed the free spirit of the earlier British Church, and could only by degrees be brought to acknowledge the authority of Boniface as their bishop. Secondly, what was of far more serious and more lasting consequence, Boniface at his consecration bound himself by an oath of ecclesiastical obedience to the Pope, similar to that taken by the Italian bishops belonging to the several patriarchal dioceses of the Roman Church; so that the German Church was placed permanently in subjection to the Bishop of Rome. We must not be too hasty in condemning Boniface for taking this step. Those were days when men were glad enough of any central authority to sustain them, and we who know the bitter consequences of the Papal Supremacy must not pass judgment upon those who unconsciously helped to build it up, as if they could foresee the future and know what we know.

For the second time Boniface was now at Rome, and could tell, not of what he hoped by God's blessing to do, but of what God had already done by his means; and for the second time he started to return across the Alps, a bishop now, encouraged by the recognition of his labours, and more than ever confident that God would speed what he had in hand. But, careful as ever to avail himself of all outward means to help him in his work, he went a second time with letters of recommendation to the Mayor of the Palace to ask his protection as before, and again Charles provided him with a safe-conduct. Probably, however, when the great man had done this he gave himself little further concern in the matter, and made small show of interest in it, and the bishops, even if they had been many times more zealous than they were, would have seemed lukewarm to the fervid missionary. Disgusted with their coldness he started with speed for the scene of his former labours in Hesse.

There he found a state of things which perhaps put him in mind of the words of Scripture, "they feared the Lord, and served their own gods;" for the dread of their old superstitions had been heavy upon his converts, and they had made a wild mixture of the new faith and the old idolatry; they still worshipped their sacred trees and fountains; some of them still offered sacrifices upon their old altars. The wizards and soothsayers still maintained their influence, and the trembling worshippers still acknowledged the might of their charms and the truth of their omens. The visible objects of superstitious worship, such as groves, rocks, and streams, had acquired a power over them which enthralled their senses and their imagination. Accustomed from generation to generation, and from the earliest childhood of each individual, to look upon them as the actual embodiments of a supernatural presence, they could not get rid of a dread which had become part of themselves. Even those who had been led to see the vanity and nothingness of idols felt all their old terror rush upon them anew as they entered a consecrated grove or looked upon the venerable trunk of a tree, which they had been taught from infancy to worship as a direct manifestation of God.

Boniface determined to strike a blow which should at once bring this matter to a distinct issue. He would show that the fear of the Lord was a stronger thing than the dread of the gods. But this must not be done in a corner. His deed must ring through the land and declare with trumpet tones that the idols are nothing and the dread of them is a lie. At Geismar, not very far from Fritzlar, in Upper Hesse, there was an ancient and gigantic oak-tree, sacred to Thor, the god of thunder. It had for generations been regarded by the people with the deepest reverence and awe, and it was chosen as a central spot for popular gatherings. The oldest man in the country could not remember a time when he had not looked with fear

THE FALL OF THOR'S OAK.

upon this outward sign of Thor's dreadful presence. Many a time had Boniface felt that this ancient tree seemed to have an irresistible power to counteract the effect of his sermons. Often as he preached upon the vanity of idols, often as his words seemed to find their way to the hearts of his hearers, so often were the new converts drawn back again to their idolatry by the mysterious fascination of Thor's consecrated oak. The grove in which it stood had been hallowed for ages to the Thunderer, and now it began more than ever to be looked upon as the sign and symbol of his might.

This oak must be destroyed publicly, solemnly felled to the earth, and that, too, by the hand of a Christian, and in the name of the living God. Boniface resolved to do it. He would break the evil spell for ever. Attended by a few of his clergy, and letting his purpose be well known beforehand, he repaired to the spot with an axe. The pagan people looked upon it as a distinct trial of strength between their ancient gods and the God of the stranger. They assembled in multitudes to watch the issue, but they stood in profound silence. It was not for them to interfere. Thor had no need of their help; the axe would be certain to recoil and bring upon the heads of the enemies of the gods the death which they deserved. The first blow fell, and a thrill of horror ran through the crowd, but Thor suffered it in silence. Another, and another, and another—but only the wind was heard among the groaning branches of the tree. Presently the ancient oak came crashing down by its own weight, and the dry trunk was shattered into four huge pieces. The spell was broken; Thor could not, or would not, save himself. Nothing remained but to bow before the superior might of the stranger's God. Before the impression of the event had time to lose its first force Boniface took the very timber which had been worshipped as a god, and built with it a Christian chapel, and called it the Church of St. Peter.

An act like this, which in any case required the utmost courage and boldness, would have been impossible without the external support with which Boniface had been careful to provide himself in the protection of the Frankish ruler, and it would have been certain to be followed by a reaction of violence against himself. Still we must not suppose that Boniface relied only or chiefly upon outward helps, or was content with producing a merely outward submission to Christ. He deeply felt the greatness and responsibility of his calling as Bishop of the

German Church, and in this way he speaks of it in a letter to an English Archbishop. " The Apostle calls the priest an overseer; the prophet calls him a watchman; the Saviour calls him a shepherd of the Church; and all agree that the teacher who is silent when he sees his people sin incurs the guilt of the blood of souls. So that a great, a dreadful necessity is forced upon us that we should be patterns to believers. Every teacher must so live as not to rob his words of their power by an inconsistent life; and, while he watches carefully over himself, he must be ready, lest he fall into condemnation, to speak to others of their sins; even as the Lord said to the prophet, *Hear the word at My mouth, and give them warning from Me.*" " It is said in the Scriptures, *The name of the Lord is a strong tower; the righteous runneth into it, and is safe.* Let us, then, stand fast in righteousness, and arm our souls against temptation, and bear what the Lord gives us to bear. Let us trust in Him Who has laid the burden upon us. What we cannot bear by our own strength let us bear through Him Who is almighty, and Who says, *My yoke is easy, and My burden is light.*"

His fatherly care for the instruction and training of his converts is touchingly expressed, towards the close of his life, in a letter in which he urges on the Frank court-chaplain, Fulrad, to provide for the continuance of his work after his death. "I entreat our Sovereign (Pepin, now King of the Franks), in the name of Christ the Son of God, that he would say during my lifetime what reward he will give to my scholars after I am gone. For in many places there are priests who have come from other lands to serve the Church; there are monks who have been placed in our cells to teach the children to read; there are aged men who have lived with me a long time, and helped me in my work. For all these I am anxious, that after my death they may not be scattered as sheep without a shepherd, and that the people who live close to the heathen may not lose their knowledge of Christ. My clergy, who live near the pagans, are often in great straits. They can, indeed, obtain daily bread, but clothes they have none, nor means of obtaining any, except what hitherto I have myself been able to send them."

After the decisive event in the grove at Geismar the heathen were far more ready to listen to the teaching of the missionaries. Churches everywhere rose, and here and there a monastery was settled. But the want of labourers was great, and Boniface sent to his native land for further help. The call was abundantly answered; a number of active and pious men flocked to him from England, and many devout women obeyed the impulse, and either founded or filled convents, which began to rise in the districts beyond the Rhine.

In this way fifteen years passed since Boniface went the second time to Rome and Gregory II. consecrated him Bishop. The Church in Germany had taken firm root, and it was time that it should be more completely organized, and take its permanent shape. Once more Boniface visited Rome. There was a new Pope now, Gregory III. Gladly he listened to the tale which the missionary had to tell, and he appointed him Archbishop and Metropolitan of the German Church, so that he had power to erect bishoprics where bishoprics were needed, and to do whatever else seemed best for the good of the Church. Next spring, 739, he returned to Germany, and immediately set to his work ot organization. One bishopric after another was founded, and a new impulse was given to the work of evangelizing men in all parts of Germany. At a council held under the new king, Carloman, the seat of Boniface's own archbishopric was fixed at Mentz, or Mayence.

Ten years more, and Boniface's threescore and ten had come to an end. Most men would have rested from their labours in the power and dignity which now surrounded him. But power and dignity were never his ruling passion. His work in Germany seemed to be over; at all events, what remained might safely be left to other hands. But it was not so elsewhere; there still lingered in his heart the memories of his first beginning as a missionary and his painful parting with Wilbrord. That work had slumbered since Wilbrord died, and the darkness had been encroaching upon the light. Why, now that his own work was done, should he not give his latest days to Friesland? He could fix upon more than one to take his place in Germany; he would go where he was wanted more. He decided upon Lull, one of the Englishmen whom he had invited into Germany, to be Archbishop in his place, and took leave of him thus:—
"I cannot but do as I am doing; I must go whither the influence of my heart leads me, for the time of my departure is at hand; soon shall I be freed from this body and obtain a crown of eternal glory. But you, my dearest son, complete the founding of the churches which I have begun; earnestly warn the people against error; complete

the building of the church in Fulda, and let that be the last resting-place of my weary body." He took with him a chest of books for him to read or sing while travelling, and a cloth in which his body was to be wrapped to be brought to Fulda.

Old man as he was, he seemed to be filled with a fresh inspiration, and he travelled through Friesland with youthful vigour, preached, converted, and baptized. But his time was drawing near. The persons who had been baptized, and who had dispersed to their homes, were all appointed to assemble on a certain day to receive confirmation. In the meantime Boniface and his companions pitched their tents on the banks of the Burda, not far from Dockum, on the borders of East and West Friesland. When the morning dawned Boniface waited with anxiety for the arrival of his converts. At length a sound was heard of an approaching crowd. But it was not the newly-baptized; it was an armed host of furious heathen, sworn to murder the enemy of the gods. Boniface had around him a number of Christian youths who were eager to fight in his defence. But he forbade them, saying, "Cease fighting, for we are commanded to return good for evil. Long and earnestly have I desired this day, and the time of my departure is come.

Be strong in the Lord, and bear whatever He sends." Then to the clergy, "Be not afraid of them that kill the body. Rejoice in the Lord and hope in Him." All met their doom.

So he received at last the crown of martyrdom. It was the 5th of June, 755. His body was afterwards brought to Fulda, as he wished.

Who that ponders the work which he did does not feel himself moved to join in the words of a modern German writer, "Blessed from generation to generation be the name of Winfrid the Anglo-Saxon"?

GREGORY AND STURM.

ST. BONIFACE, like Columban, left behind him a series of disciples who had caught the spirit of their master during his lifetime, and who laboured on in the same manner, each in his own diocese, or parish, or monastery. They devoted themselves to preaching the Gospel, to educating the young, to clearing and cultivating the soil, and gradually, though slowly, civilizing the people.

The lives of some of these have come down to us. They are full of interest, showing us still more in detail the nature of the work which was done in those days, and helping to fill up our picture of Boniface himself. One of them shows, in a remarkable manner, the fascinating and attractive power which he was able to exert over the minds of young persons.

When he had bidden Wilbrord farewell in Friesland for the second and last time, and was on his way to his own field of labour in Hesse and Thuringia, he came into the territory of Trier, or Treves, and was journeying through that valley of exuberant richness and fertility which is watered by the Moselle. He stopped at a monastery near Treves, and met with a warm and hospitable reception from the Abbess Addula. She was a woman of noble birth, who, like so many others in those times, had become weary of worldly pomp and show, and had retired into a religious house to lead a life of quiet usefulness and prayer. Her grandson, Gregory, a boy of fifteen, had been placed under her charge, and had just returned from his school at another monastery, when Boniface appeared.

It was a very prevalent custom in religious houses, both in those times and long after, that during meals one of the community should read some passage of Scripture aloud to the rest. Addula, proud perhaps of the cleverness of her grandson, fixed upon Gregory to do this when Boniface was there. And as soon as Boniface had asked a blessing upon the supper, Gregory began to read aloud out of the Latin Bible. Boniface was struck with the intelligent countenance of the boy, and when he had finished he called him and said, "You read well and clearly, my son; but tell me, do you understand the meaning of the words?" The boy, not quite catching his drift, replied that he was quite sure he understood what he had been reading. "Then tell me how you understand it." Gregory began to read over again the same as before, but Boniface stopped him, saying, "No, my son, I know very well that you can do that; but I want you to tell me in German what you have just read in Latin." The boy confessed that he could not. "Would you like me, then, to tell you what it is?" The boy was curious to hear, and Boniface then let him read the whole over again distinctly, and then he himself translated it into German, and preached upon it to the whole company. The manner and words of Boniface made upon Gregory an impression which never could be effaced. In after years he related the whole incident to his own pupil Lindger, who tells us, "It was evident from what source the words of Boniface came; for they pressed with such rapidity and power upon Gregory's mind, that at this single exhortation of a teacher whom he never saw or heard of before, he forgot his parents and his native land, and at once went up to his grandmother and begged to be allowed to go with this man and learn from him how to understand the Holy Scriptures."

The Abbess tried to keep him back, telling him that Boniface was an entire stranger, and that he was undertaking what he did not understand, and knew not whither he was promising to go. But "many waters cannot quench love." Her words were wholly in vain; Gregory adhered firmly to his sudden resolution, and said "Follow him I will; if you will not give me a horse to ride, I will follow him on foot." Then she was persuaded that something heavenly must have touched his heart; she gave him a horse and servant and bade him farewell. Lindger adds, "It appears to me that at that time the same spirit was working in this young man which inspired the Apostles when, at the word of the Lord, they left their father and their nets, and all that they had, and followed their Redeemer. This was the work of the Supreme Worker, the same Spirit of God Who works all in all, dividing to every one severally as He will."

From that time Gregory followed Boniface wherever he went; he shared all his dangers and toils, and could never be separated from him. He was with him on his perilous journey over the Alps and through Lombardy to Rome, and while Boniface was busy there on the great purposes of his mission and his training, Gregory was busy too, searching for manuscripts of the Bible and books of devotion, that he might purchase and carry them away for after-use. Rome and England were the two great storehouses of such treasures, and the opportunity was too valuable to be lost. Even at the last, when Boniface resigned the Archbishopric of Mayence, and went to preach the Gospel among the savage Frieslanders, Gregory followed him still. He was detached from him for a little space while in that country, for some cause connected with the objects of the mission, and in that short interval before they met again his master received his crown of martyrdom on the banks of the Burda.

Bishop Eodan, of Utrecht, had been with Boniface on that bright fatal day of death and life, so that the church of Utrecht, the head-quarters of the Friesland mission, was left without a pastor. As soon as Gregory received the tidings of what had happened he repaired to Utrecht and took upon himself the whole care of the mission; not, however, as bishop of the see, but simply as head of the monastery. Here he had an ample field of work congenial to his spirit, in preparing missionaries and teachers. Young men from France, England, Friesland, Suabia, Bavaria, were sent to him for education, and many of them caught from him the glow of his ardent spirit; so that the monastery became a nursery of the kingdom of God, and from this spot preachers of the Gospel went forth, not only to the neighbouring Friesland mission, but in various directions, among tribes that were still heathen, or others that had but recently received the Gospel. When a bishop was needed for Utrecht itself he did not feel himself called to the office, nor had he any desire to undertake its responsibilities, but he got episcopal consecration conferred on Alubert, an English clergyman who had joined him in his work.

In this way he lived and laboured on, carrying with him to the last the fervent zeal and stedfast purpose which had brought him in his boyhood to follow Boniface, not knowing whither he went. Early every morning he used to sit in his cell, waiting with the anxious solicitude of a father to receive the difficulties and perplexities which some of his scholars were sure to bring to him; for they knew that any one of them who needed counsel or encouragement was certain of a welcome, and would not fail to receive the blessing of a father's wisdom and a father's love. He made them feel that the Word of God was a light to their feet and a lantern to their paths, for he showed them how some portion of that Word was exactly suited to the need of the moment and to the peculiar wants and disposition of every one of them.

In his sermons he was perpetually charging his scholars to maintain with all their might the ceaseless battle against the world, the flesh, and the devil within their own hearts, for the new man could make no real progress unless the old man was continually dying. With reference to this he often quoted the words of the prophet Jeremiah, "I have set thee to root out, and to pull down, and to destroy, and to throw down, to build, and to plant;" and when he wished to encourage them to the conflict his favourite promise was, "Eye hath not seen, nor ear heard, neither hath it entered into the heart of man to conceive what God hath prepared for them that love Him."

When he had just completed his threescore years and ten a stroke of palsy deprived him of the use of his left side. But he continued as cheerful as ever, and was carried about by his scholars wherever his presence was needed, to preach, to explain the Scriptures, and to give counsel and encouragement to separate individuals. At last he was confined to his bed, and he begged that some of the Psalms might be sung to him. He never lost his consciousness, and in his last hours his disciples gathered round his bed to hear his latest word of exhortation. They comforted each other by saying, "At all events, he will not die to-day." But he gathered his remaining strength and said, "To-day I shall surely have my release." His scholars carried him into the church, which was close at hand, and he prayed and received the Holy Supper, and passed away to his eternal rest. This was in 784.

The most conspicuous of the disciples of Boniface, after Gregory, was the Abbot Sturm. He was descended from a noble and Christian family in Bavaria, and Boniface was already engaged in organizing the Bavarian Church, when his parents committed Sturm to his charge, to be trained for the spiritual office. It was impossible at that time for Boniface to undertake the charge in his own person, but he placed him in the monastery of Fritzlar, one of his earliest foundations. He would be well taken care of there by the Abbot Wigbert, and to him was entrusted the boy's education. When Sturm's education and training were complete he was ordained deacon and priest, and he then joined Boniface himself, and continued with him, assisting him in his preaching, for three years.

But he had a particular work before him, for which in due time his calling came. After the first three years had passed he was seized with a desire of following the example of others who had retired into the wilderness, not to fly from duty and the claims of human brotherhood, but to till the earth and subdue it, and point the way to civilization and the arts of peace. He wished to found a monastery somewhere in those wilds which then covered Germany, and which were reclaimed only by the transforming power of men actuated by the Spirit of the Gospel. As Boniface looked upon such monastic institutions as the best means of improvement both for the people and the land, he was well pleased with the proposal. He hoped to make use of Sturm as an instrument for converting into a cultivated country, the vast wilderness which then, under the name of Buchwald, covered a large part of Hesse. He joined with him two of his companions, and when he had prayed for them and given them his blessing, he bade them farewell, saying, "Go into Buchwald; may God enable His servants to prepare a settled habitation in the wilderness!" So they started on their way.

For two days they wandered through the forest,

riding on their asses, and seeing nothing but the ground beneath their feet and the thick gigantic trees which hid all things else from view. On the third day they came to a place which they thought might answer their purpose, and which seemed capable of cultivation. It was afterwards called Herschfeld. They called on Christ to give them His blessing, and that this place might be an abode for them, and they built for themselves little huts, which they covered with the bark of trees, and remained there a little while.

Then Sturm remembered that his dear master, Boniface, was never content with merely the convenience of the moment, but before he allowed a permanent settlement he was sure to take account of the minutest details, the situation of the place, the quality of the soil, the springs of water; for a great work was before him, and he must not waste the power which God allowed to him in ill-considered projects and attempts which might afterwards have to be given up. So he went back to ask his sanction. Boniface heard his story, and at first gave no opinion. He let him rest, and he spoke of other things; then he told him plainly, but gently, that it would not do; he must start again, and search. The place he had found was excellent in itself, but there was one fatal objection: it was close to the country of the heathen Saxons, and was constantly exposed to their ravages. A settled habitation there was impossible.

So Sturm went back to his two companions and told them what the master said, and again they started on their search. Long and vainly did they seek, wandering up and down on the Fulda, for a place which might prove suitable. At length his two companions were wearied out, and left him; and for many days Sturm roamed the forest, entirely alone, singing psalms as he went, to strengthen his faith and cheer his heart. Wild beasts were prowling round, but he feared them not. When night came on he cut down branches from the trees and made a hedge of fire round himself and his ass, to keep off the beasts of prey; then he called upon the Lord, and lay down upon the earth to sleep. One day he was suddenly startled by shouts of menace and insult from the midst of the forest, and presently he found himself in front of a troop of wild Slavonians who had been bathing in the Fulda, and who asked in mockery whither he was going. He quietly answered, " Farther into the forest;" and when they let him pass unmolested he felt that the hand of God was with him.

At last he found a spot which Boniface, when he heard of it, entirely approved; and here, in 744, the foundation was laid of the famous monastery of Fulda; and here the cultivation of the great wilderness commenced; and here, too, as generations came and passed away, the most distinguished teachers of the German Church in following ages were trained.

This was Boniface's favourite foundation. He spared no pains to make it perfect. He sent Sturm to study the patterns of the old conventual institutions, and particularly of Monte Casino, the parent monastery of the West, and he bade him gather all the information he could for the benefit of the new German foundations. After his return he was appointed the first Abbot of Fulda. He no longer followed Boniface in his labours, but settled at his monastery and entered zealously upon the task which he had all along felt that God had marked out for him. Here he dwelt, and for a long series of years he directed the energies of four thousand monks; and gradually by their unsparing labours the wilderness was reclaimed and brought into a state of cultivation.

At a later period his work was often interrupted by the devastating inroads of the Saxons, with whom, after the accession of Charlemagne, the Frankish Empire was constantly at war. It was the Emperor's earnest desire that he should preach the Gospel among these wild people; but preachers of the Gospel coming in the train of an armed host were not likely to find a very ready entrance to the hearts of men, and Charlemagne's designs were much more political than evangelical, so that no real progress was made. Often in his old age Sturm was compelled to seek a precarious safety in flight from the infuriated heathen, and returned to find his land desolated and his storehouses plundered.

On one of these occasions he was suffering from severe illness, and when at last the heathen had retired and his return was possible, he felt that his end was approaching. Charlemagne sent him his own physician, Wiatar, but his medicines seemed to do harm rather than good. At length, growing still more feeble, Sturm caused the convent bell to be rung to summon the monks to be near him and to pray for him. When they were gathered round him he exhorted them to abide faithfully in their calling, and to dwell together in love. He begged them to forgive him if he had ever wronged any one of them, and added, "For myself I forgive with all my heart all who have ever injured me; Lull, too, who has been my constant enemy." This was Archbishop Lull, whom Boniface had appointed his successor at Mayence. Between him and Sturm there had been many warm disputes, and probably faults on both sides.

Next day, the 17th of December, 779, the hand of death was visibly upon him, and he passed away in the midst of his people.

For a very long time the stream of missionaries continued to flow from England to the Continent. It seemed as if the Anglo-Saxons of our island could never forget the debt which they owed for the message of the Cross, and could never cease to use their utmost efforts to repay it.

ANSCHAR.

HITHERTO we have seen the light of the Gospel slowly but surely penetrating the darkness of Central Europe, and the messengers of the Cross were in every case either English themselves, or urged by an impulse which came from our island. We must now turn our eyes farther North, and watch the beginning of a mission in a land with which we are closely connected, but to which the Gospel came not from the Church of England, but from the Franks who had hitherto mostly looked on in indifference while others were reaping a harvest for Christ at their border.

More than a generation had passed since St. Boniface had died, when Anschar was born on the 8th of September, 801. Never was there a greater contrast between two men, never a more conspicuous instance of the manner in which the most opposite characters have their distinct but equally glorious work to do in the kingdom of God. In Boniface we have seen a character which reminds one of the Apostle Peter, ardent, impetuous, sometimes overbearing, able and eager to accomplish great things, to strike strongly and see an immediate effect of its efforts. In Anschar we see more of the quiet, unobtrusive love of St. John, calm, steady strength but also lowly self-distrust.

When he was five years old Anschar lost his mother, but even upon a child of five years old an impression may be made which can never afterwards be effaced. His father sent him to school, and mixing with other boys he soon seemed to lose all memory of the holy atmosphere of his early childhood. Yet from the very beginning he seems to have been one of those silent, contemplative lads, who, though they may enter eagerly into boyish sports, can never give themselves wholly up to them, they are haunted by feelings of a different kind, and a sense of emptiness and vanity puts a dash of bitterness even into the sweetest cup of pleasure. A voice which speaks to them alone seems to them to be perpetually calling them onward and upward. Dreams both of the day and of the night are sure to visit lads like these.

And while he was at school, Anschar had a dream which he never forgot. He thought he was in a slippery place, full of mud and mire, and as often as he tried to escape from it he slipped back into the midst of it again. But not far off he saw a pleasant path where there was no mire, but the ground was firm, and on the path was walking a beautiful woman, richly adorned, and others were with her, dressed in white garments, and among them his own mother who had loved him when he was a little child. When he saw them he longed to reach them; but the more he struggled the more firmly the mire seemed to hold him fast, and he could not get free. But the women approached nearer, and she who seemed to be the chief cried to him and said, "My son, wilt thou come to thy mother?" And when he answered eagerly that this was his heart's desire, she said again, "If thou wishest indeed to come to our company thou must give up all vain and wilful ways, and with all thy heart follow after better things." And he awoke. But the dream had a lasting effect upon his conduct.

Not very long after this, when he was thirteen, the world was startled by the news of Charlemagne's death. That the mighty monarch of so many kingdoms must lie down and die, and his pomp and power pass away from him as if they had never been, was a thought which brought home to his mind, more than ever before, the nothingness of this world and the absorbing greatness of the world unseen.

From the school where he had been placed at first he was sent to complete his training at the great Abbey of Corvey, near Amiens. But his waking thoughts by day still fashioned the dreams which visited him in sleep. He thought he was carried to the company of the blessed. And his soul was ravished with the sweetness of the heavenly song. The faces of all were turned to the East, and in the East there was the brightness of an exceeding light, which shone upon all, and shone through all, and seemed to sustain all by the attraction of its beauty. Peter and John took him by the hand and led him forward, and a Voice came from the excellent glory, saying to him, " Go hence, and come back to Me, wearing the crown of martyrdom." But he saw not the face of Him who spake to him.

Another time he thought that he was in the chapel praying, and One entered whose eyes were as a flame of fire. And he felt that it was the Lord Christ. And He said, " Confess thy sins that thou mayest be justified." And Anschar answered, " Lord, Thou knowest all already; nothing hid from Thee." And the Lord said again,

"Yea, I know all things, but I will that men confess their sin, that they may be forgiven." And Anschar confessed and prayed. And then the Lord said to him, "Fear not, I am He Who blotteth out thy transgressions." And he awoke.

There is not the least reason to doubt that these accounts are true. They are said to come from Anschar himself, and they help to show us the character of the man. To some men such things are natural and almost matters of course, while to others they seem strange and incredible. We can see at once that Anschar in later life would be either an idle self-conscious dreamer, or a man of strength and courage, whose activity would be sustained and freshened by the air of eternity.

In this monastery he remained until he was called to a more independent sphere of action. Charlemagne had been anxious, before his death, to found a monastery within the territory of the conquered Saxons, experience having shown that this was the most effectual means of spreading Christianity in the country. Not seeing his way to this he had contented himself with bringing Saxon youths to be educated in the monasteries of France that they might return as teachers to their own country. The Emperor Louis the Pious, however, resolved to carry out the original idea, and it was determined to found a monastery in a beautiful valley on the west bank of the Weser, east of Paderborn, in Westphalia. As the monks who founded it were drawn from Anschar's monastery of Corvey, near Amiens, the new foundation was called by the same name, New Corvey. Anschar was one of these monks. To him was entrusted the direction of the school of the new convent, and it was another of his duties to preach to the people, and in this way doubtless he was being prepared for his future work.

And now that work was beginning to grow visible. Harold, king of Denmark, had been baptized at Ingelheim in 826, and was returning home from a visit to his ally the Emperor Louis the Pious, and the Emperor was looking for some zealous preacher of the Gospel to accompany the Danes to their native land. But every one to whom he proposed the task was alarmed at the reports of their savage barbarism and the cruel character of their idolatry. At length when the Emperor put the question in an assembly of prelates and nobles, Wala, Abbot of Corvey, remembered Anschar, "I know of a man of glowing zeal, who longs to suffer for the cause of God." Anschar was summoned and declared himself ready to go. He was warned to consider carefully what he was undertaking, but his resolution was fixed. In the interval before he started, men began to fancy that he was shrinking from the dangers and toils before him, and repented of his promise. Not so, he was serious because he was earnest, silent because he was listening to a voice calling him, thoughtful because he was busy in inward preparation for his work. In a little while he retired to a neighbouring vineyard, to prepare himself in solitude, by prayer and study of the Scriptures, for his great undertaking. He was sought there by Autbert, one of the monks, whose heart was stirred by the sacrifice which he was making. He asked him whether his mind was still bent upon the mission. Anschar replied, "When I was asked whether I would go among the heathen in the Name of God to preach the Gospel, I could not possibly decline to obey the call. Yes; with all my heart I am still determined to go, and none shall make me waver." It ended in Autbert accompanying him, but of the other monks not a single one would entertain the proposal for a moment, and Wala would not, in such a case, interpose his authority.

The Emperor called the two missionaries before

him. He gave them church vessels, tents, and whatever else they needed for their journey, and sent them away exhorting them to zeal and perseverance in their calling.

At first they met with no very favourable reception from King Harold. It was not at his request that they were sent, and he was not disposed to pay them much respect; and the Danes, who were his followers, were a rough and barbarous set of men. But Anschar's character was exactly of a kind which could meet and cope with all this; his unwearied patience, his winning love and steadfast faith, before very long began to have their effect, and he succeeded in inspiring Harold in particular with something like affection for himself.

Anschar spent two years in Denmark, but for some unknown cause his biographer passes over this period in comparative silence, and such accounts as exist are very vague and indefinite. One thing alone can be depended upon as showing something of his work. In those barbarous times there were always great numbers of unfortunate lads to be found who had been torn from their homes in childhood, who knew no parent, brother, sister, or relative of any kind, and whom no one owned except as a slave. Anschar purchased as many of these lads as he could; others were presented to him by Harold. He took them under his care, showed them the first glimpse they ever knew of human love and sympathy, and began to educate and train them as teachers for their countrymen. He commenced with small beginnings. He was only able to start a school for twelve boys, and even for these it was difficult to find a tolerably safe place of abode, for he was in the midst of savage and cruel idolaters. At length, however, he fixed upon a spot close to the boundary of the country, at Hadeby, or Schleswig.

Months passed by, and Harold became more and more unpopular with his own people. He had offended them by the alliance which he formed with the Franks, and he had offended them very much more by being baptized as a Christian and introducing Christian missions into the land. At length they finally rose against him and drove him out of the country. There was now no restraint for their savage ferocity; it was impossible for Anschar to maintain his ground. To add to his distress, he was now entirely alone, for his only companion, Autbert, had a short time before been compelled by sickness to return to Corvey, where he soon afterwards died.

But exactly at this moment, when his work in Denmark seemed to be forcibly brought to an end, the door leading to the more remote regions of the North was suddenly opened before him, and he could not but once more recognize the calling of God. By intercourse with Christian nations some seeds of Christian knowledge had already been scattered in Sweden. As has often happened, both before and since, commerce was made the means of bringing blessings higher than itself. Christian merchants had conveyed the knowledge of the Gospel to Sweden, and merchants from Sweden, who traded with Dorstede in Friesland, which was now, since the labours of the Utrecht missionaries, a Christian country, would have heard it preached there, and some of them no doubt embraced the faith. Others, induced by what they heard from these on their return to Sweden, betook themselves to Dorstede on purpose to obtain a better and more accurate knowledge of a message which seemed so divine. Again, in the expeditions which these Northmen made to distant Christian lands, to plunder and to ravage, they often brought away with them numbers of Christian captives. And by all these means the knowledge of the Gospel had already found its way to Sweden, and attracted, more or less, the attention of the people. And so it came to pass that certain envoys, sent from Sweden to the Emperor Louis the Pious on other business, informed him that many of their countrymen at home were anxious to learn more about this thing, and they invited the Emperor to send them teachers. Louis referred the matter to Anschar, who replied that he was ready to engage in any enterprise which might glorify the Name of Christ.

Accordingly, he was appointed ambassador from Louis the Pious to the King of Sweden. He left the monk Gislema to watch events in Denmark, and seize any opportunity which might offer itself of reviving the mission there, and set out in a merchant vessel carrying valuable presents from the emperor to the king. As he was crossing the Sound the ship was attacked by pirates, and with difficulty they managed to escape with their lives. Anschar lost everything he had with him, including the priceless treasure of forty books. Many of the crew were now for abandoning the voyage; but Anschar would not hear of the proposal. He had made up his mind, he said, not to return till he had discovered whether it was God's will that he should preach the Gospel in Sweden. At length they landed at Birka, or Biorka, on the Lake of

Malarn, a port near the ancient capital, Sigtuna, and not far from Stockholm.

The voyage had been long and dangerous among the myriads of rocky islets which stud the coast of Sweden, and when at last they landed it was only to enter upon a series of perils of a different kind. Although there were some to whom his presence was most welcome, and who received him gladly, yet the great mass of the population was violently opposed to the message which he came to deliver. His friends advised him to use the presents which he had brought with him from the Emperor, in order to rescue his life from the fury of the people. But he replied, "I would give nothing here to redeem my life. If it be the Lord's will, I am ready to suffer tortures or death itself for His name's sake." He invited the king to an entertainment, and gave him the presents. No one ever knew better than he how to become all things to all men, and the fascinating charm of his manner, such meekness combined with such strength, won the heart of the king; and by degrees a way was opened before him by infinite wisdom even where at first the work had seemed most hopeless.

He easily obtained permission from the king to preach the Gospel and to baptize all such as were willing to embrace it; and he discovered a great number of Christian captives, whose hearts were filled with joy at hearing once again the voice of their home and of Christian love, and partaking once again of the Supper of the Lord. Among the first who embraced the Gospel was Herigar, a man of rank, and the governor of one of the departments of the kingdom. He became a zealous promoter of the faith, built a church at his own cost on his own estate, and used all his influence to make the Gospel known.

Anschar resided in the country for a year and a half, and met with a success which exceeded his warmest and most sanguine hopes. At the end of that time it seemed to him that a firm foundation was laid for the Church of Christ in Sweden, and he determined to return to the Frankish kingdom, and report to the Emperor Louis what had been accomplished. The account which he gave of the condition and prospects of the Church in the North was so encouraging that the Emperor resolved to carry out the plan already projected by his father, Charlemagne. He founded an Archbishopric at Hamburgh, to be the centre of operations for all the northern missions. The archbishop was to be the guiding and directing spirit of the whole, and to visit personally each separate department of the mission as he might see occasion. Anschar was the first Archbishop. As his diocese was perpetually exposed to the inroads of the heathen tribes of the North, Louis bestowed upon him the monastery of Thoroult, in Flanders, between Bruges and Ypres, both as a place of refuge in time of need, and as a source of revenue to defray expenses. The special care of the mission in Sweden was entrusted to a missionary named Gauzpert, who was to reside in the country as bishop, and on whom the monastery of Welna was bestowed for the same purpose as Thoroult had been granted to Anschar.

Anschar's labours were not in the slightest degree lightened by these changes, and his cares and anxieties were more than doubled. In Denmark the mission was for the time entirely suspended. King Horick, a violent enemy of the Gospel, reigned supreme after the expulsion of Harold, and Anschar would only endeavour to prepare the way indirectly for operations in the future. He purchased boys of the Danish, Norman, and Slavonian races; and such as he found suitable for his purpose he either kept near himself, to be trained as monks and clergy, the future teachers of their countrymen, or he sent them to be educated at the monastery of Thoroult. In Sweden, on the contrary, things at first went better. Gauzbert met with a very favourable reception; the people seemed readily to listen to the preaching of the Gospel, and for many years he laboured with good success. In the year 845, however, there was a sudden and unaccountable insurrection of the maddened heathen populace, and Gauzbert was attacked in his own house, robbed of all he had, and driven away, and this mission also seemed at the moment to be extinguished.

Exactly at this same time Anschar's own more immediate work at Hamburgh itself was threatened with destruction. The Normans entered the country, laid the whole land waste with fire and sword, and attacked and plundered the city. They seemed to make the churches and the clergy the special objects of their fury. Anschar with extreme difficulty escaped with his life, but not without losing all that he had. After years of effort he had managed to build a magnificent church and monastery: these were now burned to the ground before his eyes, and with them the library which had been given to him by the Emperor, and which could never be replaced. He looked on and saw the fruits of long years of frugality and toil vanishing into nothing as in a moment, and he kept repeating over and over the words of Job, "The Lord gave, and the Lord hath taken away; He hath done what seemed to Him good: blessed be the name of the Lord!"

He fled with some of his companions and scholars, and wandered up and down for a long time in uncertainty and sorrow, till at last he found a refuge at Rameshoe, in Holstein, on the estates of a noble lady named Ida. From this spot he travelled over his pillaged and wasted diocese, labouring to confirm the faith and console the spirits of his unfortunate people. To add to the gloom of the time, he had lost his powerful protector, the Emperor Louis, who had died in 840; and in the division of territory consequent on his death, Anschar was deprived of the monastery of Thoroult, which had hitherto sustained him in his poverty. Many of his associates left him now for want of the means of sustenance; many returned to the monastery of Corvey. But Anschar kept up heart, and bravely maintained his position, trusting in God, and hoping for days when the sun would shine again.

Thus he laboured many years, travelling from his place of refuge through every part of his wasted diocese. He was bent upon winning over to the faith King Horick of Denmark, who had taken a principal part in the incursions into the territory of Hamburgh. He got himself appointed ambassador from Germany at Horick's court; and he won his confidence to such a degree that the king admitted him to his private councils, and refused to treat with any other envoy. There is no evidence that the king himself ever embraced the Christian faith, but he was led to hold it in great respect. He allowed Anschar to lay the foundation of a Christian Church, and to establish Christian worship wherever he chose, and to baptize all who desired it. The town of Schleswig, situated on the borders of the two kingdoms, had now continual intercourse by trade with the Christian towns, Dorstede and Hamburgh. Anschar fixed upon Schleswig for the foundation of the new church. Many concealed Christians, who had been baptized at Dorstede or Hamburgh, now ventured to make public profession of their faith. Christian merchants came to the place with greater confidence, and the prosperity of the town was largely increased; and as it was the chief inlet of foreign produce into the country, the Christian character of Schleswig tended greatly to spread the knowledge of the Gospel in the inland districts.

In Sweden the work of the mission was completely suspended for seven years after Gauzbert was seized and driven out of the country. It was impossible for Anschar to recommence it himself, and he could discover no one able and willing to undertake it. At last he heard of a priest named Ardgar, who had become a hermit and devoted himself to a life of solitude and seclusion, that he might, without interruption, improve himself by prayer and study. He prevailed on this man to give up the life which he had chosen, and to engage in more active labours for the kingdom of God, and he pointed out to him the field of work which was open to him in Sweden.

Ardgar, though not without reluctance, undertook the task; and Anschar sent him away with his blessing, and begged him, as soon as he reached Sweden, to seek out Herigar, and attach himself to him. He counted confidently on the assistance which would come from Herigar's zeal and devotion, and he was not deceived in his expectations. During the seven years of spiritual famine Herigar had kept his faith alive by prayer and communion with God. He had boldly let his own belief be known, and lost no opportunity of proclaiming steadfast endurance. And several circumstances had combined to attract the attention of the people to what he said. Some of the chief of those who had taken part in the attack upon Gauzbert's house and the plunder of his goods seemed to be pursued by constant misfortune. One was the son of a chieftain, and he had carried a large portion of the booty to his father's house; soon afterwards he died, and by degrees the family was reduced to poverty: they were faithful worshippers of the gods. What could be the cause of their fall? Their own priest declared that it must be the anger of the Christian's God which was heavy upon them. Again: Birka was threatened by a hostile army, and the people sought protection from their gods in vain. Herigar seized the occasion to bid them ask help of the Lord Christ. They met together in a field, and vowed to Him a fast and a distribution of alms in his name, if He would deliver them from the enemy. They were actually delivered, and Herigar never allowed them to forget what had happened.

All this ensured a hearing for Ardgar when he came to preach the Gospel among them; and we may imagine the delight of the brave Herigar, who for seven years had not received the Lord's Supper. Through his mediation Ardgar obtained permission to preach wherever he pleased; and besides him there were many other Christians, who had painfully felt the want of a minister of the Gospel, and were not a little rejoiced at seeing one again among them. Next year, however, Herigar died, receiving in his last moments Holy Communion at the hands of Ardgar; and at his death Ardgar, who had done violence to the whole bent of his mind in undertaking the work of a missionary, now lost heart when he found himself deprived of the sympathy and support which had hitherto sustained him. He could no longer resist his longing for the quiet of the contemplative life, and he returned to his former seclusion.

Anschar's perplexity was extreme. It seemed as if the Mission, which had originally begun in so hopeful a manner, was destined never to prosper. Now that Ardgar had deserted his post, who was there to step in and fill the gap? His disappointment was the more bitter because King Horick of Denmark, now his warm friend and supporter, promised to lend his aid and protection to the work, so that the sun seemed ready to shine if any labourer could be found to reap the harvest. But who was the labourer to be? Some were kept back by fear, others by sloth. He knew not which way to look. Which was the most important, his own work at Hamburgh or this deserted field in Sweden, of which the thorns and the briars seemed to be so rapidly regaining possession? It was a difficult question to answer. He sent to Gauzbert. Would he go back and resume the work in which, seven years ago, he had been so violently interrupted? But Gauzbert replied, that after all that had passed, no one was less likely to meet with a favourable reception than himself, and, on the other hand, who so likely to be listened to as Anschar? All their remembrances of him were pleasant and friendly.

This answer of Gauzbert's chimed in exactly with a misgiving which was already in Anschar's mind, that he ought himself once more to direct, in person and on the spot, the Swedish mission; and, as had been usual with him in his youth, the thoughts which filled his mind by day reappeared in dreams by night. Adalhard, who in days gone by had been his abbot at the Corvey near Amiens, and to whom no doubt the ardent youth had often confided his visions of missionary enterprise, appeared to him in a glorified form with a message from God. The islands and the nations afar off were to hear from his lips the word of salvation;

he was destined to carry the Gospel to the utmost ends of the earth, and "*the Lord would glorify His servant.*" This dream he thought was a sign that the work to be done in Sweden was to be done by himself, and the last words he took to be a promise that a crown of martyrdom would be his reward.

But while he distinctly made up his mind that martyrdom was the probable result of the work he was undertaking, he was not one of those rash spirits who rush eagerly forward to court danger and seize the crown before it is offered. He neglected no precaution which prudence suggested. He obtained a special commission from King Louis of Germany as ambassador to Sweden, and he carried with him a letter of introduction from Horick of Denmark. "I am well acquainted," said Horick, "with this servant of God. Never in all my life have I seen so good a man, or one so worthy of trust. I have let him order everything in my kingdom as he pleases with regard to his religion, and I advise and beg of you to do the same; for he will certainly wish to do nothing but what is good and right."

Armed with these credentials he set out from his diocese in 853, not knowing what would befall him, but with his usual unwavering trust in God.

When he landed at Birka he found the people in a state of great excitement. After Ardgar's departure the greatest efforts had been made by the adherents of the old religion to destroy and stamp out the new faith. One person in particular proclaimed himself a special messenger sent by the national gods to protest against the insult which had been offered to their worship, and to demand atonement. Others again were anxious to admit Christ as a deity of proved and undoubted power into the list of the objects of their worship; and the retort was ready, "If we must have a new deity, let us not bow before the God of the stranger, but worship Eric, one of our ancient kings."

It was when the strife of tongues was at the highest, and the hope was smallest that the still small voice of the Saviour would obtain a hearing, that Anschar landed at Birka. His friends advised him to fly without even publicly announcing his presence. If he ventured among the people at such a time he would scarcely escape with life. But he replied as he had replied before, that he would abandon no enterprise merely to save his life; he would be only too glad to give it up for the cause of Christ. Yet he coupled prudence with his firmness. He invited king Olof to a feast in his own house, and displayed the presents which he had taken care to bring with him. The wonderful power of fascination, which he had already exerted with so much effect upon Horick of Denmark, began to tell upon the king of Sweden, and before the feast broke up, a beginning was already made of personal goodwill and confidence.

Anschar seized the first opportunity to ask permission to preach the Gospel in the country. Olof was inclined to grant the request, but was too cautious or too timid to do so on his own authority. He must consult his people, he said, and their gods. He first consulted his nobles, Anschar meanwhile fasting and praying that the door into Sweden might once more be thrown wide before him, and waiting in hope and fear to know the result. The nobles dared not decide without inquiring the will of the gods. The lot was cast, and word came that the gods had pronounced in favour of the preaching of Christ. Next the matter was laid before the assembly of the whole people. Some spoke on one side, some on the other; and the debate was carried on with greater and greater eagerness and heat. A tumult was beginning and blood seemed likely to be shed, when a very aged man stepped out into the midst and told how the God of the Christians had been singularly propitious to him, and had shown that He was a God of great power and might. He had saved him, and many others who had prayed to Him, from pirates and from the perils of the sea. "Many of us," he concluded, "have thought it worth while to travel over a dangerous sea to Dorstede, to learn more of this God; why should we turn away his messenger when He brings the knowledge of Him, and offers it to us at our very doors?" The old man carried the whole assembly with him, and it was resolved that free leave should be given to preach the Gospel throughout Gothland; churches might be built and the Christian worship celebrated without molestation. The same resolution was not long after adopted by the rest of the Swedes.

Olof granted Anschar a piece of ground to build a church, and he purchased another near it to build a house for the minister. Great was his joy and thankfulness at seeing so speedy an answer to his prayers, and the Mission set on foot with so fair a prospect of success. He felt that the first perils were passed, and the continuance of the work might now be left to other hands. The Danish Mission and his own people at home required his care. He had brought with him Erimbert, a priest whom he knew and trusted. To him he committed the Church in Sweden, to guide and direct the public worship, and he himself returned to his diocese in 854.

It will have been seen that Anschar's mode of conducting a Mission was wholly different from that of Boniface. Under the protection of his own monarch the latter founded as it were an alien colony in the country which he wished to evangelize. He erected a monastery as a fortress in which his missionaries could be in a measure secure from the attacks of barbarous tribes, and the community cultivated the surrounding land, introduced the arts of civilization, as well as preached the Gospel to the neighbouring tribes. Anschar, on the other hand, endeavoured to effect his purpose through the king and the principal persons of the country to which he went. He enlisted them as far as possible on his side, obtained distinct liberty to preach in the country, and then threw himself among the people apparently as one of themselves, with no other protection than the law and custom of the country or the influence of the chief men might supply to him.

He was particularly anxious that the missionaries whom he sent should follow the example of S. Paul, and ask nothing of any one, but support themselves by the labour of their own hands, together with such supplies as he himself might be able to send them from time to time. But his own means were limited and precarious. His own diocese had but lately been rescued from paganism, and he had continually to contend against violence and rapine. Yet his presence never lost its fascinating influence upon those with whom he was thrown. Manly courage and humble self-distrust were never more marvellously combined in one person. Men felt that in yielding to him they were doing homage not to himself but to some spirit of holiness which dwelt in him but was not he; hence their pride was not abased in doing his bidding, for they knew that his own pride was never flattered by their obedience.

The more they felt the beauty of his holiness the more they were persuaded that miraculous power must be at his command if he chose to exert it. Sick people were brought to him from distant places to be healed by his prayers, and nothing could convince them that he did not possess the power which they attributed to him. But of himself he said, "The one only sign from heaven which I would ask of my Lord God is that of His infinite pity He would take away my sin and make me partaker of His holiness."

When he was in his sixty-fifth year, and after he had laboured more than thirty-four years for the salvation of the heathens of the North, he was attacked by his last illness. For nearly six months he was weighed down by very severe and almost continual bodily pain. But amidst it all he kept repeating the words of Job, " Have we received good from the hand of the Lord, and shall we not receive evil?" "All that my God lays upon me is less than my sins deserve." His only regret was that his early dream of a crown of martyrdom was apparently not to be fulfilled. To the very last his mind was full of concern for his diocese, for those who stood around him, and for the Danes and Swedes who had been his care through life. And during his illness, when he felt that his end must be drawing near, he wrote to King Louis and to the German Bishops, earnestly entreating not to allow the work to cease after his departure.

At last, on the third of February, 865, he received the Lord's Supper, and immediately afterwards he lifted up his hands towards heaven, and prayed that the grace of God might pardon every one who had ever done him wrong. As his strength was ebbing away he frequently repeated the words, " Have mercy upon me, O Lord, according to Thy loving-kindness. Be merciful to me a sinner. Into Thy hands I commend my spirit." And looking steadfastly towards heaven he passed away from this world.

Slowly and steadily the work which he had begun in Sweden continued to advance until the whole kingdom was converted to the faith of Christ, and the light of the Gospel began to spread into Norway. But it was not till a century and a half had passed after his death that English missionaries were sent to complete the conversion of Jutland, and Canute the Great was reigning at last over two united Christian kingdoms of England and Denmark.

THE TENTH CENTURY—ADALBERT OF PRAGUE.

WHEN Anschar died it was already twilight in the History of the Church. It soon became midnight. It would be difficult to find a period darker than the tenth century which was about to commence. The gloom was so terrible, iniquity was so abundant, love had grown so cold, that the few who were looking for the signs of the times felt as if the end of all things must be close at hand; the knot could never be untied by human skill; the trumpet of the Archangel would soon be heard calling men to the final judgment. For centuries past men had been becoming more and more accustomed to look to Rome for health and strength, and very often they had found what they sought. Rome had often fanned into a flame sparks which were perishing in the surrounding cold, she had often held out a hand to strengthen the feeble steps of those who were tottering in their solitude. But no light or healing was coming from Rome now.

THE TENTH CENTURY—ADALBERT OF PRAGUE. 151

One after another the Popes had lately been a scandal not only to the Church but to the world. It was a shame even to speak of the things which were done of them in secret. "Woe unto the world because of offences" were words which often came to the remembrance of thinking men in those dark days. The seed of the Word, which had been sown so plentifully through Western Europe, and which had promised such a luxuriant harvest, seemed likely to be altogether choked by the thorns and thistles of violence, lust, and greed.

And when the salt has lost its savour, what taste can it impart to other things? It is only when the Church herself is rich in the gifts of the Spirit, that she either knows or cares to be the channel of those gifts to others. Only when the fountain itself is full can the water of life flow freely to spread the blessing through the world around. So we hear very little of heralds of the Gospel in that dreary period, and nothing at all of any sustained and systematic effort to win men to the faith.

But the night was not without its stars; and here and there was one who shot a bright momentary ray across the gloom, and spent his life to save the souls of men, yet left no visible work behind him, for the dawn was still far off.

Such an one was Adalbert, Bishop of Prague, whom men learned afterwards to call Apostle of Poland and Prussia. He was born at Prague, in 950, of a noble Bohemian family, and early destined for the ministry of the Church. There was at that time no University or Christian seminary of note in Bohemia, and the children of wealthy or noble families were of necessity sent to a distance for education. But the cathedral school of Magdeburg had lately become celebrated, and was daily winning a wider reputation under the direction of the famous teacher Otriko. To this school the youth was sent by his parents, who placed him under the special tutelage of Adalbert, first Archbishop of Magdeburg. The Archbishop soon learned to feel for his young pupil a deeper and more endearing interest than that which arose from this special connexion; for his moral character was elevated and his progress in the school was rapid. He had hitherto been known by his family name of Woytech; the Archbishop prevailed upon him to give this up, and substitute for it his own name Adalbert, by which he became known in history.

The relations of Bohemia to Germany were soon such as to open a career of conspicuous usefulness to a young man of Adalbert's abilities and position. The country had been conquered by force of arms, but Otho the Great, who occupied the imperial throne, felt that the conquest was insecure unless some powerful spiritual influences could be brought into action to aid the merely outward authority of the Government. He is not the only one of the great men of the world who have tried to use the Gospel of Christ as an instrument of their own ambition, or for merely political ends; nor is he the only one who has been miserably disappointed by the result. He determined to found a Bishopric at Prague, and the Bishop was to be one of the numerous suffragans of St. Boniface's successors, the Archbishops of Mentz. But who was to be the bishop? Who could be found to unite in himself the many qualities necessary for such a difficult position? He was expected to win Bohemia to the faith of Christ, but above all things to aim at strengthening the power of Germany; he was to be in heart a German, but in language and outward show Bohemian. At last a priest named Diethmar was found and chosen for the post; he was born in Saxony, but spoke fluently the Slavonian language. He had no sense of the contradiction of his position, for he was absorbed in a third object which Otho had never contemplated, and was more anxious to accumulate wealth for himself than either to promote the interests of the Emperor or the spiritual welfare of the people entrusted to his care. He died in 982, mourning on his deathbed that he had chosen his portion in this world, and found it vanity.

But his tears could not wash away the evil he had done. The Bohemians now not only identified the Gospel of Christ with the foreign yoke which they detested, but identified it farther with covetousness and the love of money. They were no nearer submission to Germany than they had been before; and they were farther from Christ than ever. No one who knew much of the world was likely to covet the succession to the Bishopric of Prague; the difficulties of the position would daunt the merely selfish, the double allegiance would repel the single-hearted. For some little while the See was vacant. At last there was found one whose life had hitherto been passed in a cathedral school, and who knew little of the ways of men. His knowledge of the world was small, his enthusiasm was great. This was Adalbert. He was at that age when men think little of difficulty, nothing of danger. Ready to dare all things for the cause of Christ, he did not consider, for he did not distinctly perceive, the complications of the position to which he thought himself called. To the German Court he seemed to have been created for this very crisis, and already marked out for the vacant post. Bohemian by birth, German by education, who could be better adapted than he to extend the civil and ecclesiastical influence of Germany in Bohemia?

Once thought of, there was no hesitation about his appointment. Otho the Great was dead, but Otho II. was carrying out the same policy upon the Imperial throne. In 983 he held a summer Diet at Verona, and during the session Adalbert appeared. He had been sought out at Magdeburg by a little party of persons interested in Bohemian Church and State, and in their company he crossed the Alps, and was presented to the Emperor. Without delay he was at once invested with the episcopal staff and ring, and on the 19th of June he was consecrated Bishop of Prague by Willig, Archbishop of Mentz, and quickly set out for his native city to win Bohemia for Otho and for Christ. He thought that the one service would be included in the other. He meant to be a faithful soldier of the Cross, and he imagined that this would in itself extend the sway of his earthly sovereign. He found that it was impossible. No man can serve two masters, and he was soon compelled to choose between the one and the other.

His choice was speedily made. He must do the work of a bishop in the Church of God. That was his first and greatest vocation. But the false position was a constant source of vexation and pain. His conscience was distracted by opposite obligations. He had taken an oath which, if he kept it, would compel him to be false to his country, and prostitute his holy calling for political ends. This constant strife and irritation within himself made it more impossible than ever for him to acquire what he most sorely needed, practical wisdom and tact in the management of men. When he found himself in the midst of a people who were baptized Christians in name and profession, but heathen in manner of life and in most of their religious ceremonies; when even the clergy loved to have it so, and were themselves living in open profligacy and were themselves even outwardly half heathen still, he could not endure the contradiction, and was for enforcing submission by the mere exercise of authority. But neither clergy nor people would submit to his control. His earnestness and zeal produced no better impression than the selfishness and greed of Diethmar. At last the fightings without and the struggles within his own heart became greater than he could bear, and in despair and disgust he fairly fled from his post, uncertain whether to seek some other sphere of missionary labour, or to look for rest and peace in a monastery. But he was compelled to go back to the flock he had forsaken, and he continued with them awhile. Again he left them and again he returned. At length, for the third and last time, he took his departure. Otho III. released him from the promise which was torturing his conscience, and he never returned to his native city again.

To put the hand to the plough, and afterwards to draw back is a serious thing, even when the first step was an error; the original mistake cannot be entirely corrected by merely retracing our steps; our moral strength has received a wound, our firmness of purpose is weakened. Such was Adalbert's experience now. He was no longer what he had been. He was still as determined as ever to spend himself for Christ, but the glow of enthusiasm which had first carried him to Prague had lost something of its impetuous strength. He could not endure the thought of the inactive life of the cloister, and yet whither should he go? What was the work which God had for him to do?

Neighbouring Hungary had begun to call itself Christian, but only because Prince Geisa had married a Christian wife, and she had persuaded him to be baptized. Adalbert determined to go and see what further impression he could make. He could make none, and again he turned away from the work he had undertaken, disappointed and perplexed.

Now the thought came to separate himself for ever from other men's labours. He had been thwarted and turned aside by the example, the policy, the plans, the persuasions of others; he would go where no Christian man had ever been before, and strike a blow for Christ in some yet untrodden field. Prussia was heathen, savage, barbarous; what a crown of glory it would be to bring the Prussians to the Redeemer's feet! And so at last he turned to what seemed to be his proper work, and to a sphere of labour where he was to leave behind him an example only bright.

Between him and Prussia lay the great kingdom of Poland, where Boleslav I. was doing for the

Poles what Henry the Fowler and Otho the Great had done for the Germans, giving them a firm and settled government and welding them into a nation.

Help from Boleslav at the commencement of his enterprise would be like the opening of the door which would lead him to his future work, a pledge and an earnest of success. All went well. Boleslav not only encouraged him in his purpose, but placed a royal vessel at his service, and gave him thirty armed men for a guard. He started full of hope. His pupil Radim was with him and a priest named Benedict, and the three sailed together down the river Weichsel, with the strange soldiers round them, and the country growing more and more monotonous and dreary as they floated on. At last they reached Dantzic, the border-town of civilization, where Poland ended and Prussia was to begin. Here he considered that his ministry began. He must preach the Gospel at Dantzic, and perhaps afterwards God would lead him farther. So he stayed and preached and baptized, but not for many days. The unwonted feeling that God was with him indeed, and that at last his work would be blessed, was filling his heart with hope and strength.

Dantzic is at the western extremity of that gulf

of the Baltic to which it gives its name. The eastern portion of the gulf is called the Frische Haff, and is almost converted into a lake by the long low sandy line of the Frische Nehrung, which, sweeping in a wide curve to the north-east, carries the eye to the promontory of Bruster Head, beyond which again, but out of sight, is the next of the little Haffs, which, separated from the open sea each by its own tongue of land, are almost continuous in this part of the southern shore of the Baltic. Bruster Head and the country round it were in those days called by the name of Samland. The city of Königsberg stands there now, at the mouth of the river Pregel, but no city stood there then; it was a shelterless inhospitable coast, and inhabited by tribes whose hearts were as savage as the wild winds which unceasingly swept the shore.

Elate with the first successes of his preaching, and with a heart full of the glad consciousness of his apostleship, Adalbert stood on the shore at Dantzic, and looked across the gulf to the barren waste of Samland. He felt mysteriously attracted thither, and it seemed to lure him on, and invite him to enter upon a victorious path of which he had as yet scarcely taken the first step. He would commit himself at once and for ever to the work before him; he would deprive himself of all possibility of again drawing back; at one stroke he would offer himself an entire sacrifice to Christ.

His resolution was taken. A return was at any time open to him from Dantzic, and Dantzic, if for no other reason, must be left behind him; he would plunge into deep waters from whence there could be no returning. Boleslav's orders had been that he should be taken whithersoever he chose to go; so the little vessel was again prepared and the crew made themselves ready, not knowing what was before them. Their task was over sooner than they perhaps expected. Adalbert had determined to trust no longer to human aid. The pagans should see that he relied only on the protection of God; his manifest faith in the unseen should be the first beginning of his teaching. The little vessel was to carry him across the gulf and then to leave him for ever, him, and his pupil Radim, and Benedict the priest.

None disputed his will, and slowly they sailed eastwards; on their right was the long low barren shore of the gulf; in front of them was the long low strip of sand which is the Frische Nehrung; on their left the open waters of the Baltic. They landed at last on a dreary beach, no tree or human

L

habitation near; it seems to have been the northern extremity of the Frische Nehrung. Here the crew received his blessing and started on their voyage back, leaving him and his two companions on the barren shore, alone and fearless, leaving also a little boat, to be used when occasion required.

The Frische Nehrung was not a place where they could continue long, even if they wished it so; and between them and the mainland now was only the narrow water of the Frische Haff. They launched their little boat, and rowed across the waves. Just where the Pregel flows into the sea there was a little island which, to one approaching from the west, seemed like a little circle of land, enclosed within the double mouth of the river, and forbidding to ascend the stream. On this island they landed. Signs of human habitation were there, and the boat had been seen as it approached the shore. The natives came down to receive the strangers, to receive but not to welcome. Their appearance was ominous of evil; their gestures were threatening; and they were armed with cudgels. Adalbert landed with his psalter in his hand, singing psalms of trust and praise and holy cheer. A native seized one of the oars of the now forsaken boat, dashed the psalter from his hand, and felled him to the ground. He recovered himself, looked up to heaven, and cried, "I thank Thee, Lord, that Thou hast counted me worthy to receive a blow for the dear sake of Him Who died for love of me."

Here they seem to have met with no further molestation. And on Saturday they crossed one of the mouths of the Pregel to a spot on the coast of Samland. The chief man of the district came down to the shore to meet them. When he saw that they were men of peace, and were not carrying arms, his curiosity was excited; he received them kindly, and without many words he took charge of them, and led them to his village. Their arrival was quickly noised abroad, and a great multitude of people ran together to see and to hear. Who could they be? whence had they come? The vessel which brought them to the Frische Haff had not been seen from the mouth of the Pregel. Could that little boat have brought them from distant lands across a stormy sea? for in look and bearing and gesture they surely were strangers and foreigners. When Adalbert had told them his name and his country they were nearly as ignorant as ever. But he mentioned the name of Boleslav, and that name was well known to them already;

it was mixed in their minds with hope and fear and dim dreams of power and wealth.

And then Adalbert went on in a gentle tone to tell them for what purpose he had come. "I have come to bring salvation to this land. I call upon you to turn away from your idols which have no life, which have ears but cannot hear, which have mouths but cannot speak, and to bow down before Him Who made you, the only living and true God, for beside Him is none else; and His Name, through faith in His Name, shall give you eternal life, and you shall become partakers for ever of everlasting joy."

When they heard these words they became full of fury, and gnashed upon him with their teeth. Some of them lifted their cudgels and threatened to take away his life; others rushed upon him and beat him with sticks. But they were awed by the presence of the chieftain who had brought him there, and no further violence was done. At all events, they cried, let him be thankful that he had so far escaped with life; if he wished to save his head let him fly that very night. In that country men had one law and one custom; whoever should be found, by the morning light, speaking of another God and another law, he should surely die.

So Adalbert and Radim and Benedict the priest were hurried away to the shore, and forced into their little boat, and compelled without delay to put out to sea. That same evening they landed again at another spot on the same coast. Here they found another little village, where they were less inhospitably received; and they abode there five days.

On Friday morning Adalbert's pupil Radim told him of a dream which he had had the night before. "I saw," he said, "on the middle of the altar a golden cup standing, and it was filled half up to the brim with wine. No one was there watching beside it, and I thought myself alone. I went up to the altar to drink of the wine; but then a servant of the altar came and bade me touch it not. That wine, he said, was neither his nor mine to drink. It was for the Bishop alone. To-morrow he was to drink of it and receive strength." Adalbert thought within himself that the vision pointed to his crown of martyrdom. But he only said, "Dreams, my son, are treacherous things; put no trust in the visions of the night. If indeed it come from God, may His blessing rest upon it." And when the day broke, they went on their way.

As the sun rose higher and higher in the heaven they travelled farther and farther on their way; they made a path for themselves through the thick pathless forest, where there was no track of man's foot to guide them. Nothing seemed to weary them, nothing to make them afraid. It seemed as if their singing gave them a strength beyond their own, and the praises of God gave them courage. For as they went they were making the woods echo with their hymns of thanksgiving. First one, and then another, and then all three together, raised the song of faith, "We praise Thee, O God; we acknowledge Thee to be the Lord;" and it seemed to them like a shout of victory in the very stronghold of sin. And they sang again how, when He overcame the sharpness of death, He opened the kingdom of Heaven to all believers; and their thoughts were so fixed upon their heavenly Home, that they took no note of the hours as they passed, or of the length of the way.

But they had travelled many a mile, and the morning hours were gone. At last they reached the other side of the forest, and came out into an open space where there was much grass and some fields. The sun was high in heaven: it was noon. Here they stopped; Radim broke the bread in the

MARTYRDOM OF ADALBERT.

Name of the Lord, and blessed the cup; and Adalbert partook of the Lord's Supper. Was this the wine which was to give him strength? was his crown of martyrdom near him now? They found out now that they were tired and hungry, and they sat down on the green grass, and began to eat the food which they had brought with them. Then Adalbert repeated some words of Scripture, and again they sang a song, and started on their way once more; but they had not gone far when they were overcome with fatigue; they lay down upon the soft turf, and all three soon fell into a deep sleep.

How long they lay there they never knew. They were startled out of their sleep by the sudden shouting of an angry crowd. Adalbert had trodden, or from a distance he had seemed to tread, upon a sacred shield. The gods claimed him for their own; his blood must wash out the insult. All three were seized and thrown into chains. Adalbert, even in earlier days, had never lacked the courage to do and to dare when the path of duty was plain. Now, without fear for himself, he laboured only to strengthen his brethren. "Let not your heart be troubled. If we suffer, it is for the Name of the Lord, the King of kings, and

Lord of lords, the source and fountain of grace, the altogether lovely. Good and beautiful it is to offer our life a sacrifice to Him Who is so sweet."

Siggo, the priest of the false gods, was one of the crowd. When he heard the words of Adalbert he became frantic with rage. He snatched a spear, and rushed upon him, and plunged it madly with all his might into his breast; and others followed, covering him with wounds. Radim and Benedict the priest looked on, and when they saw him lift up his eyes to heaven in the midst of the murderous blows, they knew that he was praying that every one of that multitude might be saved alive from sin. They themselves stood in their chains waiting for their own turn to come. But it came not. They were kept close prisoners for many days, till, at last, Boleslav heard of it, and ransomed them from captivity.

It was on the 23rd of April, 997, that Adalbert received his crown of martyrdom. Afterwards, when men began to call him Saint and Apostle of Prussia, a mangled body was brought from the Pregel, and laid in honour in the Church of Gnesen, in the Duchy of Posen; and pilgrims came to worship, and the sick to be healed of their diseases, at the shrine called by his name.

There is something very sad in the thought of Adalbert's life and death. From his youth up he was striving restlessly to do something great for God; but from his youth up he seemed to strive in vain. Except those few sunny days in Dantzic he seemed to accomplish nothing. His work bore no visible fruit at Prague, in Hungary, or in Prussia. He was one of many such who lived and died in that dreary century. Over the Church in general a thick gloom was spread. Iniquity abounded, and love was very cold. Here and there some solitary spirit caught a glimpse of a higher life. But even those who did so stumbled in the darkness, and could scarcely find their way. Hardly they kept alive the spark of love within themselves; amid the depth of the surrounding cold it seemed impossible for them to spread the flame and kindle the hearts of others. It was not a time for missions, and those few who attempted such a work attempted it alone, and failed.

The eleventh century brought better days. In other lands the message of the Gospel was spoken and received; but Prussia had still two hundred years to wait. Just ten years after Adalbert's attempt was quenched in blood, Bruno went from Querfurt with a little band of eighteen, and perished in like manner in the same region. And then Prussia was let alone for two centuries. When the work began again, it began in a very different manner and a very different spirit. Then we can scarcely recognize the champions of the Cross as belonging to the same army of martyrs. The Church was changing rapidly, and missions were changing too. The age of the Crusades had come.

But, in the interval, the tide was rising; and while Prussia was still heathen, Pomerania had become Christian.

OTTO, APOSTLE OF POMERANIA.

OTTO, Apostle of Pomerania, was a man of much more steadfast will, and firmer purpose, and larger soul, than Adalbert of Prague. He was a man, too, of swift decision, quickly discerning where his path of duty lay, and strongly setting himself to walk in it.

He was a Suabian of noble birth, but his father was not wealthy, and he himself was a younger son. This last fact, which seemed to be against him, was perhaps the source of his greatness. It supplied a spur without which his energies might have slumbered. His father gave him a learned education and left him early to himself, to make what use of it he could. The youth set his heart on becoming a student at the University of Paris, which already filled Europe with its fame, and where he hoped to win all wisdom and all knowledge. But necessity put him to a different school; all his energies must be turned, for many a year, to the one purpose of gaining a livelihood; and it was not likely to be gained at home.

He felt that his bread must be won by teaching, if at all; and where could he turn his talents and education to best account? Poland at this time was still only half Christian, and was far behind all other lands in Christian culture. It stood sorely in need of an educated clergy, and a school erected there would spread a blessing far and wide. Thither went Otto, and began to teach. His rivals were few, for none in that country could compete with him in what were then considered the essentials of a scholastic education. Children of the noblest birth were intrusted to his care, and he mixed on familiar terms with the principal men of the country. Before long, Duke Wratislav Hermann invited him to his court and made him his chaplain, and by degrees he began to be employed in political transactions of importance. The Duke had lost his first wife, Judith, and was casting about for a second alliance, when Otto, thinking of his own country, directed his attention to Sophia, sister of the Emperor Henry IV.; and he was one of the commissioners sent to the Emperor's court, to ask the hand of the princess in marriage. It was a delicate mission, but he managed it with success, and brought back the bride.

After this he was of higher consideration than

ever at the Polish court. He was frequently sent on embassies to Germany, and in this way he became well acquainted with his own sovereign, Henry IV. At last he was invited to return to his own country and become chaplain and secretary to the Emperor. Every day added to the honour and favour which was lavished upon him. He was made chancellor of the empire, and, finally, when the see of Bamberg fell vacant, in 1102, he was made bishop of that diocese.

He devoted himself to the work of his bishopric with all the zeal and fervour of his character; he preached frequently to the people in their own language, and men flocked to hear him; for the clearness of his style and the earnestness of his delivery were alike remarkable. The revenues of his bishopric were ample, and the economy and frugality of his mode of life made them more ample still, and he was ever ready to give of his abundance to the support of any good work which needed his help. Princes and noblemen, far and near, were continually making him presents, but their presents almost invariably found their way to the homes of the poor.

Many stories are told of the manner in which he used to deny himself luxuries and comforts in order to supply the wants of others. Once, in Lent, when fish were very dear, his servants placed a large one, of high price, upon the table before him. He turned to his steward, who stood in attendance, and said, "Who am I, the poor unworthy Otto, that such a dish should be placed before me? God forbid that I should swallow such a sum of money at one meal! Take it to my Christ: He is dearer to me than I am to myself. Find some one lying upon a sick bed, and give it to him. I am strong and well, and bread is enough for me." Another time some one sent him as a present a rich and costly fur, and begged that he would keep it in remembrance of the giver. "Yes," said he, "it is a precious thing. I will keep it so carefully that no moth shall ever corrupt it, nor any thief break through and steal it;" and he sent it at once to a poor lame man whom he knew. He kept by him an exact list of all the sick in the city where he lived, with notes of their several complaints and the circumstances of their condition, that he might be able to give to each exactly what he needed most; so that, in a time of famine and great distress, he was able to save the lives of many, and multitudes of mourners gave thanks for the consolation which he brought to them in their bereavement.

So Otto's life was flying by, full of good works, full of the love of God and the service of man, when one day an unexpected stranger appeared and told a tale which changed the course of all. It was Bernard. Born in Spain, and a bishop in his native land, he told Otto how he had left it to preach the Gospel in Pomerania. He had remembered the words of Jesus, how He had said, " Provide neither gold nor silver nor brass in your purses, neither two coats, neither shoes, nor yet staves," and he had thought to follow them, and he had gone barefoot, and clad in such garments as beggars use. But the people of Pomerania were rich and prosperous; they clothed themselves luxuriously and fared sumptuously, and despised the poor; and when the messenger of Christ, clad in the garments of poverty and begging his bread, came among them, preaching the Gospel of God, they said to themselves that he must have come, not to save the souls of men, but to win this world's good things for himself. They would not suffer him to remain amongst them. They had done him no hurt, but had put him on board a ship and sent him out of their country. Otto might succeed where he had failed. Wealth and talents might make an impression where lowly poverty had been despised. The Bishop of Bamberg might appear among the Pomeranians with a pomp and splendour equal to that of their own priests.

Otto listened to Bernard's tale, and the thought gathered strength that God had marked out this work for him. And soon it was confirmed by another sign. A letter came from Boleslav of Poland, son of his old master Wratislav, urging this very enterprise upon him. For three long years the Duke had been searching for some one to undertake the work of carrying the Gospel to Pomerania, but he could find none. He remembered Otto at his father's court, and he felt that he was fitted for the task. He would charge himself with the whole cost; he would provide an escort, assistant priests, and all things else, if Otto would but undertake to do his part.

The arrival of this letter fixed his resolution. The combination of events all pointing in the same direction seemed to him to be a Divine commission which he could not contradict, and on the 24th of April, 1124, he set out for Pomerania. In all respects his appearance and equipment were the exact contrary to those of Bernard. He determined to present himself in the full splendour of his episcopal dignity. He not only provided himself with everything that could be required for the support of himself and his party, but he also carried with him costly raiment and other things for presents to the chiefs. It was his object to make the Pomeranians distinctly understand that no motives of self-interest could have brought him among them.

He first paid a visit to Duke Boleslav in the city of Gnesen in Posen. The Duke was better than his word. He gave Otto a great number of waggons to convey his baggage and provisions, a large sum of money for his expenses, people who spoke German and Slavic to be his servants, three of his own chaplains for his assistants, and the commandant Paulitzky, a man devoted to the cause of the Mission, for his protector. Such an escort ensured him a fair reception from Duke Wratislav of Pomerania, who met him on the banks of the frontier river Netze, and gave him full liberty to teach and baptize throughout his whole dominions.

Next morning they crossed the border and immediately set out for the town of Pyritz, a long weary journey through a thinly peopled district. It is worth while pausing to watch what happened at Pyritz, because it shows how much the spirit of Missions had already changed, and how men had

M

insensibly been led to trust in the arm of the flesh, even while they were proclaiming the things of the Spirit.

It was eleven o'clock at night when they reached the town. But night was being turned into day. A great heathen festival was being celebrated with feasting and revelry, and the town was filled with the light of torches and the sound of song. Otto pitched his tents at some distance from the walls, and would not even kindle a fire for fear of attracting the attention of the excited crowd. In the morning Paulitzky entered the town, and in the names of the two Dukes called a meeting of the inhabitants. Some time before, after a victory of Boleslav, the people had promised that they would become Christians. They were now called upon instantly to keep their promise; instantly, for a Christian Bishop who had forsaken all he had for their sakes, was come to claim it. At that moment Otto, with his train and baggage, entered the town in state. The people were terrified, for they thought it must be a hostile attack, and that their gods had forsaken them; but when they were assured that no violence was to be feared, they submitted and listened. Seven days were spent in giving them instruction, three in preparing for baptism. For twenty days more Otto remained in the town, and seven thousand were baptized. At length he took his leave, first preaching through an interpreter to the newly baptized. He warned them of the danger of relapsing into idolatry, and explained to them the principles of the Christian warfare against sin, dwelling particularly upon sinful practices to which, as a nation, they were addicted. And he bade them farewell and left the town, which now called itself Christian.

We meet sadly often at this period with so-called conversions such as these, of towns and peoples, sudden and wholesale. And one cannot but marvel that men like Otto, who certainly knew what spiritual religion was, could be satisfied even for a moment with work so hollow and unreal. Yet he showed that he was aware of its hollowness, and he longed for and aimed at something better and more enduring.

Leaving Pyritz, another long journey across a monotonous and thinly peopled plain brought them to the town of Kammin, near the shore of the Baltic. This place was not entirely unprepared for their coming. The chief of Wratislav's numerous wives lived there. She was more nearly a Christian than she dared to confess in the midst of a heathen population, but after news came of what had happened at Pyritz she took courage to declare herself openly on the Christian side. By the time the Bishop reached the town many persons were anxiously waiting for his arrival that they might receive instruction. Forty days Otto remained there, baptizing great numbers, and when at last he went away he left behind him one of his clergy to carry on the work which he had begun.

His next attempt required greater courage. Kammin is situated on the eastern side of that great "Haff" into which the river Oder flows at its mouth, and which is separated from the open Baltic by the two large islands of Usedom and Wollin, which together form an almost continuous line from the eastern to the western shore. The islands along the Baltic coast were the seats of savage idolatry. Cut off from the humanizing influence of intercourse with others, the inhabitants of these islands were more untamed than the dwellers on the mainland, their worship was more cruel, their manners more ferocious, their resentment greater at any interference from without.

From Kammin to the island of Wollin there was but a short voyage across one of the channels through which the Haff pours its waters into the Baltic. It was quickly passed, two citizens of Pyritz accompanying Otto and his party as guides. As they approached the principal city of Julin the guides were seized with panic, and their fear spread through the whole party, Otto alone remaining unshaken in his resolve. But he yielded so far as to agree to enter the place by night, and take refuge first in the castle belonging to the Duke. But this appearance of fear made matters only worse. A furious attack was made upon them in the morning, and they were compelled to abandon their asylum. Paulitzky tried to soothe the people, but his words had no effect upon the frantic crowd, and with much difficulty he saved the life of Otto, who was thrown into the mire and trampled under foot. At last they contrived to escape unharmed from the city, but tarried five days in the neighbourhood hoping for better things. When the five days came to an end the people advised Otto to repair at once to Stettin, the capital town of Pomerania. What Stettin should do in the matter of the Gospel, that they promised that they would do themselves.

To Stettin accordingly he immediately went. All depended upon what might happen there. And very interesting and instructive it is to watch the history of Otto's Mission, and to mark the manner in which the message of the Gospel presents itself to nations of different degrees of culture, and how necessary it is that the missionary of the Cross should know how to become all things to all men. Very differently does the truth present itself to one nation in old age and decay, and to another in the bloom of its infancy. The Pomeranians were in a condition like that of children, who are not yet acquainted with the evils through which man must pass on his way from infancy to manhood.' The vices which St. Paul describes, at the commencement of the Epistle to the Romans, as so rife in the old age of the world in his day, were so far removed from them, that even the evils of commencing civilization were unknown among them. They lived in a state of primitive simplicity; they had not yet learned to deceive and to steal; they were puzzled when they saw the locks by which Otto's baggage was guarded, for nothing was kept under lock and key among themselves. Unsuspicious hospitality was the daily practice of every head of a family. They were richly endowed with the gifts of external nature; the climate was healthy, the land remarkable for its fertility. "If

BISHOP OTTO AND THE YOUNG MEN IN THE WHITE ROBES OF BAPTISM.

only the vine and the olive and the fig-tree were there, you would take the country for the land of promise," says the author of Otto's life, after dwelling upon the abundance of corn and honey and the numerous herds of cattle. There was nothing to rouse in them the sense either of physical or moral evil, nothing to produce a consciousness of sin or a longing for redemption. When they compared their own condition with others, they could see nothing to make them wish to exchange places with the Christian nations of Germany. Among the Christians, said the more respectable inhabitants of Stettin, are thieves and robbers; every kind of crime abounds among them, and punishment must needs follow crime. Christian abhors Christian: far from us be such a Gospel. These people were "alive without the law:" on their way to the higher life they must struggle with death, and be made acquainted with sin. Will they resist it, or will they become its slaves?

Meanwhile the manifest vices which they saw among their Christian neighbours were the greatest hindrance to the spread of the Gospel among them. Otto set himself with all his might to correct the evil impression and to show them a high ideal of self-sacrificing love. Alms were not needed where there were no poor, but many a captive he redeemed at his own expense, and sent him back to his friends with store of clothes and provisions. Twice a week, on market days, he came out in his robes, with the crosier borne before him, and preached the doctrines of the Christian faith. Multitudes came to listen, but week after week passed by and no candidates were seeking baptism. But in Pomerania, as in so many other countries, men, in following their own instincts of war or commerce, become unintentionally the means of spreading the kingdom of God. There were at Stettin many secret Christians who had originally entered the place as captives. Among them was a woman who had been brought from her native land while still a girl, and was now the wife of a man of wealth and position and the mother of two sons. She had never forgotten the faith of her childhood, though she had not ventured openly to avow herself a Christian. Her heart leaped for joy when the news came that Bishop Otto was coming to Stettin. After his arrival she induced her two sons to pay frequent visits to the strangers, and to ask them questions about their faith. Each visit strengthened the influence which Otto had succeeded in gaining over them; at last they declared themselves convinced of the truth of the Gospel, and begged that they might be prepared for baptism. All this was done without the knowledge of their mother, whom they supposed to be a heathen. When the appointed day came they were baptized, and for a week afterwards they remained with the Bishop; but before the week was over the mother had heard what had happened. Struggling to conceal her joy, she sent a message to Otto, begging to be allowed to see her sons. The Bishop received her seated on the grass with his clergy round him, and the two young men at his feet in the white robes of baptism. For many a year she had longed to see that sight, and now that she saw it the joy was too strong for her; it was more than she could bear, and she sank to the earth and wept. Otto and his clergy hastened to her and lifted her up, and strove to comfort her, thinking she had fainted from suddenness of sorrow. As soon as she could speak they were amazed at hearing her cry, "I praise Thee, Lord Jesus Christ, fountain of hope and source of all consolation, that I have lived to see my sons dedicated to Thee in Thy holy Sacrament, and enlightened by Thy Divine truth." And she turned to her sons and kissed them, and said, "For Thou knowest, O Lord Jesus Christ, how for these many years I have ceased not, in the depths of my heart, to commit these my children to Thy mercy, and to pray Thee to do in them that which Thou hast now done." And she turned to the Bishop and said, " Blessed be thy coming to this town. Only go on and faint not. Be not weary with waiting long, for the time shall come when much people shall be added to the Lord in this place, and a great church be built up here. Behold, I myself stand before you and confess myself a Christian, for now I know that the Almighty God will support me, and thy presence, venerable father, strengthens me, and my children will help me." As she went on to tell her story the Bishop praised God for His mercy, he encouraged her with words of sympathy and confirmed her in the faith, and sent her away with a present of a costly fur. And when the week was over and the newly baptized had laid aside their white robes, he gave them the Lord's Supper, exhorted them to be steadfast in the faith, and sent them also away with valuable presents to their home.

The conversion of these two young men was the beginning of an abundant harvest. Their mother took courage and openly avowed herself a Christian, using her utmost influence to induce her friends and neighbours to accept the faith. Her sons became preachers to the youth of their own age. They spoke of the lofty ideal of which they had caught a glimpse in Otto's life, of the new and blessed truth which they heard from his lips, of the power of life which had come to them through his words. Their zeal inflamed the hearts of others. Young men flocked to the Bishop to ask questions and to learn the words of this life. The young instructed the old; children taught their parents, and numbers every day presented themselves and begged to be baptized.

All this was very different from the beginning of Otto's work at Pyritz. There was no confusion here between the sword of the Spirit and the arm of the flesh; no wholesale admission of crowds of ignorant heathen asking for the outward sign of baptism under the pressure of a foreign power of this world. The people of Stettin had caught a glimpse of the beauty of holiness, and the power of the Redeemer had touched their hearts. They bowed down before the King Whom their spirit recognized as One Who had a right to rule over them.

But other influences were added soon. Boleslav had heard of the ill success of the Mission at the first, and once more he must needs appear upon the scene to mar the work, while thinking that he furthered it. Messengers came from Gnesen with a royal letter commanding the Pomeranians to submit to baptism and accept the teaching of Otto on pain of seeing their country wasted with fire and sword.

What the effect of this letter might have been if it had arrived at the commencement of Otto's stay in Stettin it is impossible to say. At best it would have produced a strange and perplexing mixture of motives; it might possibly have nipped the whole of the good work in the bud. But Otto's words had already found their way to the hearts of so many of the people of Stettin that the Word of God had taken firm root in the place. Otto called the people together, and bade them, now that they knew the living God, destroy the shrines and monuments of their dead idols. They could not gainsay his warnings, but they still clung to old associations around them; and though they were convinced that "an idol is nothing in the world," they dared not lay violent hands upon the temples and images of the gods. They would gladly see it done; they had not the courage to do it themselves. Otto undertook to do it for them. He and his clergy would sign themselves with the sign of the cross, arm themselves with hatchets and axes, and demolish the monuments of idolatry. When they had done this, and no harm came to them, the spell would be broken for ever.

There was a sumptuous temple richly decorated within with works of sculpture and paintings in oil. Much treasure and abundance of costly offerings were laid up there; goblets of horn adorned with precious stones, golden bowls, knives and poniards curiously wrought; for the tenth part of all the spoils of war were devoted to the great god Triglav; and this was his chosen shrine, and his image was worshipped there. Let this temple be the first sacrifice to the knowledge of the truth. The people looked on in calm acquiescence till the work of destruction was complete. But what was to be done with the treasure? The Bishop had taught them the vanity of the idol; he was the messenger of the living God; let him take the offerings for his own. But "God forbid," said he, "that I should do any such thing. I did not come here to enrich myself at your cost. Such things as these, and far more beautiful, I have already at home." He made the people divide among themselves the riches of the temple, and the only gift he consented to receive was the image of Triglav; the body he destroyed, but preserved the triple head as a trophy of the victory of Christ.

Three other buildings were next destroyed. The people had set them apart for sports and feastings in honour of the idols, and to consult under their inspiration on matters of state. The spell was weakened, but it must be completely broken; no such building could be spared. But near each of these temples was an ancient oak, and beside it a fountain. It was because of the oak and the fountain that the buildings had been reared; for these trees and these waters were the signs of the power and presence of the gods. Must these be destroyed also? The people besought Otto that they might be spared. Never should they be again associated with any sacred rites; now that the temples, the work of men's hands, which had been connected with them, were destroyed, they might remain unhurt; for were they not the work of the living God Himself? Otto hesitated, but granted the request.

On the other hand, he was immovably resolved upon the destruction of everything from which he thought that a new lease of life might be given to the dead idolatry. There was a sacred horse which was used for purposes of divination. Nine javelins were placed in a row; when any doubtful enterprise was under discussion the horse was led over the javelins; if he passed them all without touching one with his hoof the omen was favourable; it was a sign of victory. Otto was inexorably severe in insisting that the sacred horse should be destroyed or sold into another country. Such was his influence that one man alone was bold enough to resist the demand. It was the priest whose business it was to tend and manage the consecrated animal. His resistance was in vain. The horse was banished from the land. Not many days afterwards men heard with a shudder that this man had died suddenly. He alone had stood up for the honour of the idols; the living God, they said, must have passed judgment upon him.

Five months Otto remained in Stettin. When he went away he left behind him a church of living stones, a consecrated house of God for Christian worship, and a priest.

He visited some villages belonging to Stettin, and then sailed down the Oder, crossed the Haff, and landed in the island of Wollin where he was before. He had not forgotten the promise of the people of Julin, the chief town of the island.

Whatever Stettin should do in the matter of the Gospel, the men of Julin would do likewise. The Bishop went to claim the fulfilment of the promise. They were prepared to keep their word. Messengers had already been sent to Stettin, and had returned, bringing news of all that had been done there; and the citizens of Julin received the Bishop with every mark of welcome and honour. Two months he remained among them, teaching and baptizing.

The time was now approaching fast when Otto would be obliged to return to his own diocese of Bamberg, which was suffering from the absence of its chief shepherd. He became anxious for the future of the Church in Pomerania, and wished much to secure its permanence by founding a bishopric in the country. Which of its cities should be the bishop's see? Stettin seemed most suitable, as being the capital, but the presence of the chief pastor appeared to be more sorely needed among the savage people of the islands, and Julin was a convenient central point from which the whole seaboard of Pomerania might without difficulty be visited, and the more inland districts be reached in this manner. Julin, therefore, was fixed upon for a residence, but the appointment of the bishop was deferred for the present. Otto laid the foundations of two churches and departed.

He travelled to Colberg, then to Belgard, and sowed the seeds of a Christian Church in both these cities. Belgard was the farthest point which he reached in this his first missionary tour. But before he actually set out on his homeward journey he was anxious to follow the example of St. Paul, to go again and visit the brethren in every city where he had preached the word of the Lord, and see how they were doing. He went therefore through the western half of Pomerania confirming the churches. Many who had been baptized before were now confirmed; many who had been absent before were baptized; churches of which he had laid the foundation-stone were completed and ready for consecration. The brethren in each place, having felt their need of him in his absence, entreated him to remain among them and be their bishop; but it might not be. Eleven months he had spent in Pomerania, and he hastened to be with his own flock before they celebrated Palm Sunday and the Holy Week.

He returned by the same way by which he had come, through Poland: there he visited Duke Boleslav and told the tale of his successful tour.

Boleslav wished Otto himself to be the first Bishop of Julin; but this was not to be thought of. Adalbert, who had been one of his companions in the mission, and understood the work which had to be done, was nominated to the post. Otto had left a few priests behind him, but they were few in number, and none of them probably gifted with the spirit and courage which had animated himself. And though he had laid a real foundation, the building had been too rapid, the motives of many in becoming Christians had been too mixed, the time he could give to their instruction had been too short, for the work to be considered permanent and thorough. All seemed now to depend upon Adalbert. Would his strength be equal to the task?

And now one half of Pomerania was worshipping God in Christ, and one half was bowing down before the lords many and the gods many of heathen idolatry. But both looked back upon the same ancient customs, the same religious festivals, the same revels in honour of the powers of nature. Which would have the strongest power to influence the other; the new life or the old associations?

Adalbert's strength did not prove equal to the task; the old associations soon began to extinguish the new life, and the nation so swiftly won for

Christ seemed to be sinking back into idolatry. Many of those who had been baptized had only become Christians under the pressure of the tide which had set so strongly in that direction; and now that that pressure had lost much of its strength, they gave up their new profession. Many more had yielded because the God of the Christians seemed to be the stronger deity, but in their hearts they were heathen still. Many heathen priests who had become Christians were surprised and angry at finding that their old influence went for nothing and their power had gone, and they gladly welcomed any opportunity of regaining their lost positions. Many were Christians in their heart and soul and ready to die for Christ, but these for the most part led a hidden life unobserved among the multitude.

Tidings of these things came to Otto from time to time, and filled his heart with sorrow. He longed to return in person to the scene of his labours, and stem the tide of evil. But sad work was going on in Germany nearer home, and he could ill be spared. The long conflict between the great house of Hohenstaufen and the Popes had filled Germany with confusion just when she sorely needed quiet times for her own peaceful development; Church and

State alike were in wild disorder. Clearly enough Otto's place was in his own diocese.

Three years passed in this way. Otto's heart was torn two different ways; news from the north became worse and worse, while things around him showed little sign of improvement. At last, in the spring of 1128, he thought he saw his way to visit Pomerania again. This time he was determined to go to warfare entirely at his own cost; he would ask no help from Boleslav or the Duke of Bohemia. All that he needed should be provided by himself; and he would travel by a different route, going round through Saxony and the country now called Mecklenburg.

When he reached Halle he bought a very large store of corn for provision, and all manner of furs, rich garments, and precious things for presents. He had found the use of such things before at Stettin and elsewhere; they were sure to be serviceable again. All these things he put on board boats upon the Saale, to be conveyed by water to the Elbe and the Havel, after which a huge train of fifty waggons were to carry them across country to Pomerania. Demmin was the first Pomeranian town he reached, just across the frontier. The governor turned out to be an old acquaintance, but every one else was strange to him. Next day he met with another old friend, but in a manner he neither expected nor desired. Duke Wratislav had been waging war with the Leuticians across the border, and the stout old warrior was coming back; and he entered Demmin the day after Otto reached it, laden with spoils, and driving before him a great crowd of men and women whom he had made captive. All the booty, captives and chattels alike, was to be divided according to custom. There was to be a sundering of all the bonds which nature had forged and affection had riveted. Husbands and wives, children and parents, brothers and sisters, were to be torn from one another for life as chance or covetousness might dictate. What was Otto to think of such a sight as this? Here was already an opportunity to show what Christian love might do. First he interceded with the Duke, and obtained from him the free release, without ransom, of the infirm, the delicate, and the sick; next he persuaded him to give such orders as should prevent near kinsfolk and relatives from being separated from one another; and lastly, he ransomed at his own expense great numbers who were still heathen, instructed them in the Gospel, and sent them back to their homes.

Otto and the Duke were on the best of terms with each other; and the Bishop lost no time in bringing forward the subject which was next his heart, the revival and extension of the knowledge of Christ in Pomerania. Wratislav was ready to forward his views. Political motives no doubt, and the decided line which Boleslav had thought fit to take in the matter, had a large share in determining his actions; but he seems to have felt a real reverence for the character of Otto, and perhaps a genuine though imperfect appreciation of the grandeur of his Mission; and while the Bishop was present his influence was usually paramount. Whitsun-tide was close at hand, and Wratislav agreed to Otto's proposal that a Diet should at that time be held, and an effort made to bring about some common and energetic action for the establishment of the Christian Church throughout Pomerania. The Duke immediately issued letters summoning the Diet, and plainly announcing that it was not called together for any of the ordinary political purposes, but that a Christian Bishop had arrived among them to preach the Gospel, and they were called upon to decide what attitude they were, as a nation, to assume towards him.

Although Stettin was the capital of the country, and it contained several large towns besides, yet it was always felt that the true centre of gravity of the nation was in the islands; in them national feeling was most intense, and national character was least modified by influences from without. It was therefore decided that the Diet should be held at Usedom, one of the two large islands which together serve as a barrier between the Baltic Sea and the great Haff into which the river Oder flows. To Usedom therefore Otto at once set out. It was only a short distance from Demmin to the River Peene, and that stream, flowing directly eastward and entering the Haff close to the island, offered an admirable means of conveying his heavy baggage. He laded a vessel with all his goods upon its waters, and in three days it safely arrived at Usedom. He himself, however, determined to travel slowly by land. This would give him an opportunity of mixing in some measure with the people of the country, and preparing the way for the preaching of the Gospel. He took a few attendants with him, and rode at his leisure along the bank of the river, and found his baggage at Usedom, which it had reached some time before him.

When Whitsun-tide came the Diet met according to summons. The Deputies of the States were many and various, but there was scarcely a Christian among them; some of them had been converted and baptized during Otto's previous visit, and had afterwards relapsed into their old superstition; most of them had never been otherwise than heathen all their lives. The Duke introduced the Bishop to the Assembly. We are not told what Otto's personal appearance was, but we find many hints that the steadfast will and earnest purpose which ruled his character were expressed in his outward bearing, and he carried with him a lofty and commanding dignity which seldom failed to have its effect upon the minds of those with whom he was brought into contact. Nor did it fail in the present instance; the whole assembly was struck with reverence when he appeared.

Wratislav made a long and impressive speech. He called upon the Deputies of the States to set the example, each among his own people, of worshipping the living God. Hitherto they had put the question by, declaring that the preachers of the Gospel were a needy, despicable set of men, who gave no sign of being themselves believers in their own message, but who practised this craft to get their living. That excuse could avail them now no more. Here was one of the greatest prelates of the German Empire; no one could say that he was seeking anything for himself; all Pomerania could not match the wealth which was within his reach at home; he had gold and silver and precious stones in abundance; but he made himself poor for their sakes; he had given up luxury and high position, and had come to give them the treasure which he counted the richest of all.

Such words instantly told upon the Assembly. They called upon the Bishop himself to speak, and declared themselves ready to entertain any proposals that he might make to them. Then Otto rose; he spoke of the grace and truth of God in Christ, of the forgiveness of sins; of the pentecostal gift of the Holy Spirit and His life-giving power. A deep impression was made by his appearance and his words. Those who had fallen away, now declared themselves penitent, and asked to be restored to their spiritual privileges; the Bishop reconciled them with the Church. Those who had always been heathen, now begged to be instructed in the truth of the Gospel. They passed a decree unanimously permitting the free preaching of the Gospel throughout Pomerania. Otto himself continued for a week in Usedom, and then, as the whole country now stood open before him, he commenced, after the example of Christ, sending out his clergy, two and two, into all the towns and villages, intending afterwards to follow them himself, and to confirm their work.

But it is easy to make a decree, not so easy to secure obedience to it. They who had not been present at the Diet, who had not heard Wratislav's speech, who had not been under the spell of Otto's commanding influence and heard his words, were as strongly attached as ever to their old customs, and were little disposed to renounce them at the bidding of others; and besides, there were several cities of importance which only half admitted the authority of the Diet in any matter whatever, and which would be prejudiced against the preaching of the Gospel by the mere fact that it had been sanctioned by the Deputies of the States. Otto was far too well aware of the state of the country to suppose that his work was done because he had for the time convinced the Deputies. A very important step had been taken, but it was no more than a step; a long journey was still to be accomplished before the land was Christian.

Wolgast was the first town to which Otto determined to go, but first he sent before him two of his clergy, Ulric and Albin. Wolgast stands upon an island separated from the mainland by only a narrow stream, as Thanet is from Kent; but it is close to Usedom, and it shared the savage character and the cruel superstitions of the other islands. A heathen priest was living here, who for more than a year had been setting himself with an intensity of hatred to hinder in all ways the spread of the Gospel and to rouse the people to fury in defence of the ancient gods. He knew well that Christian preachers were sure to appear now that the decree of the Diet had opened the country to them, and he was resolved to make their preaching in Wolgast impossible. He had recourse to one of those pious frauds which have so often served the purpose of religionists of every kind. He went by night to a neighbouring forest, and hid himself among the trees upon a hill, by the side of which a path led to the city. Towards morning he dressed himself in the white robes of the priesthood, and waited till some one should pass by. Soon after dawn a single peasant approached on his way to the town in the morning twilight. Suddenly a voice from the darkness of the forest startled and terrified him, bidding him stand and listen, and a white figure, which to his terrified imagination seemed superhuman, showed itself amongst the trees, and by its gestures commanded attention. Again the awful voice, " I am the greatest of the gods." And the trembling peasant heard the wrath of heaven proclaimed against those who dared to listen to the name of a strange god. Those who introduced another worship must not be suffered to live. The voice ceased, and the peasant went on his way to tell his story in the city. The priest was there before him, and, affecting to doubt the tale, he questioned the credulous man, drawing more and more awful pictures from his excited imagination. The people of the town, not doubting that they had had a message from heaven, passed a decree that if the bishop or any of his clergy entered the city they should immediately be put to death, and any citizen who ventured to give them a lodging should share their fate.

Such was the state of things when Ulric and Albin entered Wolgast; they knew nothing of what had passed, and were wholly ignorant of the danger that awaited them, looking only for that hospitality which the Pomeranians invariably showed to strangers. They presented themselves first at the house of the burgomaster. His wife was well known in the town for her deeds of charity and kindness, as well as by the reverence she had expressed for the unknown God, though neither she nor her husband were Christians. She at once received the strangers into her house, and entertained them. But a very short time had passed before their talk showed plainly who they were, and they told her the object of their visit to the town. Terrified at the danger which menaced herself as well as her guests, she told them of the feeling in the town, and the decree which had lately been made; but nothing, she said, should induce her to violate the laws of hospitality. She managed to hide the strangers in the upper part of the house, and had their baggage conveyed away with all speed outside the walls. Their arrival, however, had not been unnoticed, and questions began to be asked. At any ordinary time strangers might come and go and scarcely any attention might be paid to them; even those who received them into their houses would scarcely ask who they were or whence they came. But now the people of the town were wild with superstition and fear, and suspicion was quickly roused. One after another neighbours came to inquire who these strangers might have been, but they saw no signs of their presence in the house. The woman made no secret of the fact that strangers had been there; they had had refreshment, she said, and had gone on their way, as hundreds had done before them, and as others might do to-morrow. The whole occurrence seemed so completely in accordance with the customs of the country that suspicion was soon set at rest.

The next day passed, and the next, and Ulric and Albin were still waiting for an opportunity of escape from their concealment, when an event occurred which gave them courage to show themselves. Otto was come to Wolgast, and the Duke was with him, and some of the members of the Diet, and a large band of followers, and a company of armed men. The Bishop had proposed to come alone, but tidings had reached Usedom of what the people of Wolgast were about, and Wratislav had insisted upon coming to protect him. In the presence of the Duke the city must needs be still; there was no talk now of death to Bishop or Mission-priest, or punishment on those who harboured them; the whole city was harbouring them, and the gods were slumbering or made no sign.

The missionaries who came with Otto could see

no danger in the place, and they laughed at Ulric and Albin when they told of the narrow escape which they had had from death. They were so determined to show their courage that they forgot to be prudent. They parted from the Bishop and the rest of the company, and mingled separately among the people. At last, in curiosity or mere foolhardiness, they made an effort to slip into the temple itself. Instantly the rumour flew from mouth to mouth that they were looking for an opportunity to set the temple on fire. The fury of the multitude was roused once more. The Duke and his soldiers were alike forgotten or despised. The crowd rushed, with arms in their hands, to rescue the temple of their god from the violence of the profane. Ulric was there; it was well, for had he been absent blood would certainly have been shed, and it would not have been easy to call it the blood of martyrdom. " I have tempted my God too often already," he cried; " I will not tempt Him again;" and he turned away to join the Bishop. Others, who had laughed at him before, were ready enough to follow him now. The crowd let them pass, and no harm was done to them. But one of the party, more rash than the rest, had gone too far to draw back when the others retired. His hand had already grasped the door of the temple. Encodric was his name. In one body the multitude rushed upon him. The others had escaped; here was the victim who should make atonement for them all; they would wreak their vengeance upon him. Mad with terror, and expecting instant death, Encodric fled through the doorway into the temple. The multitude paused in awe. For a few moments he ran round the interior, looking vainly for some place where he could hide himself from his pursuers. At last, looking up in his despair, his eye caught sight of something suspended from the roof, but within his reach. It was a shield, wrought with great art and embossed with gold. He snatched it from its place, and, holding it before him, he sprang into the midst of the furious crowd. None dared to touch him. He was amazed to see them part asunder before him to the right hand and the left, and make way for him as the waters of the Red Sea parted to make way for the children of Israel when they fled from Pharaoh. His life was given to him for a prey, and he seemed to be saved by a miracle. Afterwards he knew that it was the very superstition of the heathen which had saved his life. The shield was sacred to Gerovith, god of war; whoever bore it before him was safe from violence, for if any dared to touch him, Gerovith would surely avenge his death.

Otto severely rebuked Encodric for his rashness. Conduct such as his could only place in jeopardy the whole success of the Mission. He waited till he could win the hearts of the people by other and more Christian means; and before he left Wolgast they themselves had, with their own hands, destroyed their temples, and he had laid the foundation of a Christian church.

Then he went on to Gutzkow. Wratislav would willingly have been with him still, with his armed men, to protect him from the violence of the people. But the Bishop chose rather to be alone. Sometimes, as at Wolgast, the power of the Duke was needed for a little space, to secure the first beginning of the Bishop's labour; but it grieved him to be obliged to use such aid, and he made haste to dispense with it as soon as he could without actually courting danger, and to depend only upon the power of Christian love and the confidence of Christian faith. He had scarcely parted from the Duke when another offer was made to him of protection. The Margrave Albert, afterwards of Brandenburg, had heard of all that had happened at Wolgast, and sent messengers to meet Otto at Gutzkow and propose to come to his assistance. But the offer was steadily declined.

No such help, indeed, was needed at Gutzkow. The people were from the very first inclined to submit. The same mixture of motives was at work which we have already elsewhere seen. Otto was recognized as a power whom it would not do to oppose; the God of the Christians seemed to be mightier than the old gods of the land. Otto never hesitated to use the influence which proceeded from such a source. He distrusted the outward arm of the flesh, and the submission which was the result of bodily fear; but the terror of the spirit, the awe of superior supernatural power, seemed to him to be weapons which he might almost as legitimately use as that of Christian love alone.

His power was very apparent at Gutzkow. The people of the town had lately built a magnificent temple, and they were proud of the new ornament of the city; they were proud of its wealth, proud of its beauty, proud of the presence of the Deity, of which it was the outward sign and symbol. That temple must be destroyed. The people would make any sacrifice to save it; Otto was determined that it must fall. It is a curious picture which the history presents to us; the heathen upon their knees beseeching the solitary Christian Bishop to spare the idol shrine. But it could not be. The most costly presents were offered to him for a ransom, but he would not yield. Presently they changed the form of their petition. Temples had before now been converted into Christian churches. Would Otto do the same with this, and consecrate it anew in the name of Christ? But the Bishop was inexorable. "Would any man think," he asked, "of sowing good seed among thorns and thistles? Surely one must first pluck up the weeds, then the good seed may perchance have room to grow." At last he so completely overcame the reluctance of the people, that, of their own free will, and with their own hands, they razed to the ground the temple which had been the pride and glory of their town.

But Otto was not ignorant of human nature; he was well aware that a reaction usually follows any great strain; it would not do to allow the people's minds to brood unoccupied over what he had prevailed upon them to destroy. He quickly took pains to fill with something else the gap which he had made. They had pulled to the ground a stately temple; they should have a church of equal splendour. They had been proud of the one; they should have as good reason to be proud of the other. He laid the foundation himself, and hastened the erection with all speed. It was impossible for him to remain among them till the entire building could be finished; but as soon as the sanctuary was complete, and the Holy Table was in its place, he seized the opportunity of celebrating the dedication with a splendid festival. They had been used to a gorgeous ceremonial at the dedication of their temples; this should outshine them all, and the whole nation should be called upon to take part in it. The impression was to be wide and deep.

On this occasion we have exhibited to us, in considerable detail, the manner in which Otto, highly as he valued the influence of outward pomp and splendour, still looked upon them only as means to an end; and never lost sight of his main object, the winning of men's spirits to the love of God.

Nobles and common people came from far and wide to be present at the festival, and the whole of the stately ceremonial of the church was observed in their presence; and Otto then went on to explain to them the meaning of what they had seen. The outward signs, he told them, were in themselves but empty symbols; an inner truth was intended to shine through them and give them life. It would be a fatal mistake to suppose that the Gospel of Christ demanded of men only the observance of outward forms. They had been consecrating the building to be the house of God; but what, after all, was the true house of God? It was not made with hands; it was the living spirit of man; the faithful were they who recognized by faith Christ dwelling within their hearts. Let them cleanse their hearts from sin, and make them temples meet for the presence of God. In this way he dwelt long and earnestly upon the grandeur and the awfulness of heart-communion with God. The multitude listened spell-bound, and felt that his words were true.

Among them Mizlav listened. Mizlav was governor of the district. He had been present at the assembly of the States at Usedom, and took part in the decree which opened the country to the preaching of the Gospel. Otto's words at Usedom had sunk into his heart, and he had been baptized. The same voice was now to bring him to another crisis in his life. While all were listening, and all were filled with awe in presence of the searching Truth, the Bishop suddenly, in the midst of his speaking, turned and looked at Mizlav, and singled him out. "Thou art the true house of God, my beloved Son. To-day thou shalt be made holy and sacred for ever; sacred to God thy Almighty Maker. Thou shalt be separated from every other master, set apart to be His alone, His temple, and His dwelling-place. Open wide the door, my son, that the King of Glory may come in to thee. Little profit would it be to have set apart this house for His Name, if thine own soul does not also become His." Like Saul, when he heard the voice from heaven calling him by his name, Mizlav, trembling and astonished at the sudden summons, asked what he must do to prepare his heart for the presence of the Lord. Otto saw that the arrow had entered into his soul, and he perceived that the Holy Spirit was at work; and he lost no time in following up his words, and pointing the way of salvation. "In part thou art already, my son, a house of God. Already He dwells within thee, and works within thee. Thou hast had faith to turn away from idols, and to ask for the grace of baptism. See that thou complete the good work. Add to thy faith virtue, and to virtue brotherly kindness, and to brotherly kindness charity," He went on to show how falsehood and envying, covetousness and oppression, would grieve and drive away the Holy Spirit from the heart; how the Lord would dwell most dearly with those who are most like Himself, who do to others as they would be done by. If Mizlav really desired to have the presence of the Lord abiding in his heart, let him take this for the settled principle of his life, and begin instantly to act upon it; let him learn to love and forgive others as God for Christ's sake forgave him.

The strength of his resolution was immediately brought to the test. A large number of persons were in his debt, and many of them, unable to pay what they owed, were pining hopelessly in prison. Some of these last were Christians, members of the same household of faith with himself. Otto called upon him to set these last, at all events, at liberty. "This is a hard thing," replied Mizlav, "for the sums of money which these persons owe me are very large." "What if they be," said the Bishop, "has not the Lord Himself taught us to pray, 'forgive us our debts as we also forgive our debtors'? He who is ready, in the name of the Lord, to set at liberty those who are debtors to himself, he only can be sure that his own sins are forgiven." It was a hard struggle, and for a moment the issue seemed doubtful. At last Mizlav sighed deeply and said, " In the name of the Lord Jesus Christ I set at liberty all who are in prison for my sake; so that, according to your word, my own sins may be forgiven, and I may be perfectly set apart this day to be a holy temple to the Lord." The prisoners were instantly set free, and all hearts were filled with joy, and felt that that day was a festival indeed.

But there was more to come. One of the sacred vessels, which should have been used in the consecration of the church, was missing, and the most unlikely places were searched in hope of finding it. Two or three of Otto's attendants, searching for it in every direction, chanced to light upon a cell underground. A voice from within answered to the noise they made, and they found inside a young man bound in chains, who implored their help. Mizlav, he said, had bound him there. His tale was true. His father, a nobleman of Denmark, owed Mizlav five hundred pounds of gold, and had given his son as a security. It was not likely that the money would ever be paid, and the youth seemed to be doomed to a lifelong captivity. The hope of deliverance seemed now to have come to him direct from heaven. Word was instantly brought to the Bishop, but what was he to do? Could he ask

Mizlav for a further sacrifice, when he had already done so much and at such cost to himself? Yet, on the other hand, ought the joy of such a festival to be marred by the sorrow and despair of one whose heart might still be made glad? He could not bring himself to leave the youth to his doom without an effort to save him, but it seemed best to make the effort indirectly. After earnest prayer to God for guidance, he called his clergy together and bade them speak to Mizlav in their own name, speak of the sacrifices he had made, and of the Bishop's full appreciation of what he had done, and then gently ask him to crown the whole by the release of this young man. Again there was a hard struggle in Mizlav's mind. That nobleman of Denmark was the chief of his debtors, and the debt was very large; to release his son would be to give up all hope of payment. But again he yielded. With tears in his eyes he went to the Bishop and declared that the young man was free. "Yea, I will give up my own body, all that I am, and all that I have, for the dear sake of my Lord Jesus Christ." Such an example, set by such a man, had a very great effect upon the other nobles; many of them were roused to emulation and made similar sacrifices for the love of the Redeemer.

In this way Otto had gathered in the first-fruits of Pomerania for Christ. The work had been begun hopefully, and was proceeding prosperously; to his ardent spirit it seemed to be already almost accomplished. It was time, he thought, to leave its completion to other if feebler hands, and himself to push forward to new labours and new dangers. The labours were an attraction to him; the dangers were a fascination. Hitherto he had chafed at the restraints which wisdom and prudence plainly showed to be necessary; he could not refuse the protection of Wratislav while he preached the Gospel in Pomerania, and to that protection, humanly speaking, his success had mainly been owing. The outward show of earthly power had shielded him more than once or twice from violence and death. Now there came into his heart a longing to see the finger of God more plainly in his work, to trust entirely to heavenly protection and the sword of the Spirit, to cast away all earthly support, so that it might become plainly visible to all that his strength was not in the arm of the flesh but in the wisdom of God.

The longing was in his heart, and the opportunity was daily before his eyes. He almost seemed to himself to see a hand visibly beckoning him onward to a more daring and perilous work which would need all his faith and all his courage. A little to the west of Wolgast there stretches into the Baltic the promontory upon which now stands the modern city of Stralsund, and separated from that promontory by a very narrow channel is the Isle of Rugen, directly north of Wolgast, and full in view. Men might reach it in a short day's sail. Rugen was more entirely a stronghold of heathenism than even Wollin or Usedom. A small tribe dwelt there, distinct from the tribes which inhabited the mainland. They had but little communication with the people of the opposite shore; they rejoiced in their isolation, and were savagely devoted to the gods. The recent conversion of the Pomeranians had roused them to fury. They were maddened by the thought that any Christian missionary should ever land upon their own shores, and they breathed out threatenings and slaughter against the daring intruder.

Otto was well aware of all this. It allured him and fascinated him. Day after day he gazed upon the island, and day after day the belief grew stronger that this was the field which God had sent him to reap. It was white already for the harvest, and he longed to gather the wheat into the garner. There he would win his crown of martyrdom, and offer his life a sacrifice in the cause of the Redeemer. Again and again it was impressed upon him that to land on such a coast was certain death, and that to live for Christ was a nobler sacrifice than to die. He treated such arguments as the sophistry of unbelief and fear. A voice within him called him onwards, and he would not doubt that it was the voice of God. " Oh ye of little faith," he said, " must not deeds of faith and holy courage preach the Gospel with a louder voice than any words? If every one of us were to shed his blood for the Gospel's sake, and yield his life in landing on the heathen shore, such blood could never be shed in vain : it would but set a seal to the truth of the Gospel, and the faith would spread with greater power than ever."

It became a contest of opposite wills. He was determined to cross to the island; they were determined, if possible, to prevent him. He watched for an opportunity of crossing unobserved; they watched him closely to make his crossing impossible.

One of the clergy, however, shared his zeal, or else was unconsciously influenced by witnessing the strong resolve of the Bishop. It was Ulric—

Ulric whose head had been in the lion's mouth at Wolgast, and who had saved many lives by his wisdom when Encodric risked his by his rashness in the crowd at the temple door. Now he was ready to do and to dare, not in the excitement of a moment's impulse, but with sustained courage and steady resolution. He had no need to watch his opportunity of crossing to Rugen; no one set so great store by his life as to make any serious effort to prevent his running into danger. He asked for Otto's blessing upon his purpose, and the Bishop was more than willing to give it. He prepared his little boat, the smaller the better, for he must manage it by himself alone, no one was likely to share with him the perils of the enterprise. He had no baggage to carry with him, but he placed in the little boat such things as would be necessary to celebrate the Holy Communion.

He embarked, but his embarking seemed to be the signal for wind and storm to begin their work. Once, twice, three times, he was driven back by the fury of the waves, only to renew his effort once more the moment the tempest should show any sign of abating. And so for seven weary days he battled with the winds and waves in the vain endeavour to exchange the perils of the sea for the perils among the heathen on the opposite shore. Was it an evil spirit that rode the storm, that the people of Rugen might sit in darkness still? or was it God Himself Who interposed His hand? and were the wind and storm only fulfilling His word, because the time was not yet come? The hour would surely come at last; who could tell what day might bring it? So Ulric took his life in his hand, and day after day he began the struggle anew, and day after day the violence of the waves drove him back to the shore he had left.

At last another danger was added besides the fury of the storm. His little boat sprang a leak, and even in calm water it could scarcely live. Then Otto said it must be the will of God, and he tried to be content while he bade Ulric desist from any further effort. He never reached the Isle of Rugen or preached the Gospel there. There was other work for him to do; his time was not yet come, and his end was not to be as he thought.

But whether we look upon this strong desire to cross to Rugen as wise or foolish, courageous or rash, it is one of the many periods of Otto's life upon which one loves to dwell; for it is not the only one which seems to show the true devotion of his spirit, and to prove that when he appeared among the Pomeranians in the pomp and splendour of a German prelate, he was not indulging any pride or vain glory of his own, but using means which he deliberately chose as the best calculated to spread the kingdom of Christ. No one was less careful of his own dignity than he, except when the honour of God seemed to be involved in asserting it. Very few of the prince-prelates of the German Church would have borne so freely as he did the blame of those beneath him. Once when he and his clergy were dining together the conversation turned, as well it might, upon Ulric's vain endeavours to reach the Isle of Rugen, and the great risk which he ran in the effort. " Suppose he had been drowned in the waves," said one, " who would have been to blame for his death ? " " Surely," was the reply, " he is a murderer who urges another into a danger which costs his life." There could be no doubt to whom the speaker alluded. But Otto showed no resentment. He only asked in his turn, " When the Lord Jesus sent forth His disciples as sheep in the midst of wolves, was He then a murderer if the wolves devoured the sheep ? "

But now that he was compelled to give up the expedition to the Isle of Rugen, and his thoughts were forced back upon the mainland of Pomerania, he began to realize more distinctly than ever before how imperfect his work still was, and how much remained to be accomplished. It was necessary to scatter the seed of the Gospel as widely as possible over the country, so that no part of it should remain unvisited. He therefore determined to alter his plan of action. Hitherto it had been his ordinary practice to move about from place to place with all his clergy round him, and so to labour in common with them from a single point. Now, however, he determined to divide the work between them and himself by sending them to different stations.

For himself he chose the post of greatest difficulty and greatest danger. Things were not going on well in Stettin. The faith of Christ had been planted deeply in the hearts of many, and, as events afterwards showed, it had taken too firm a hold of them to be uprooted; they were ready to suffer shame for His name and to die for His sake. These persons were mostly of the higher class, men of comparative culture and education. But their devotion had not as yet been proved; and the reports which reached Otto were of a very different kind. The multitude of the city were fickle and unsteady, swayed hither and thither according to external circumstances or the changing impulse of the hour. Lately an alarming epidemic had spread in the city; it attacked both men and animals, and caused the loss of many lives. Those who were heathen still at heart knew how to profit by such an event. "Behold the anger of the insulted gods! they begin at last to vindicate their outraged honour." Such words were readily believed by the fickle crowd; their passions were swiftly roused, and they rushed to destroy one of the newly-erected Christian churches. Far and wide the rumour spread through Pomerania that Stettin was again the chief city of the gods, and that whoever ventured there to name the name of Christ would do so at the cost of his life. To all appearance the whole of Otto's work had to be done over again. He did not know of the little band of faithful men whose hearts were fixed trusting in the Lord.

It was clear that he must go back to Stettin, and that without delay. But those of his clergy whom he fixed upon to accompany him trembled at the thought, and would not be persuaded to risk their lives on such a Mission. Again and again he strove to overcome their fear, and to give them a share of his own courageous faith; but all his efforts were in vain. His own spirit never quailed for a moment. The work had to be done; if others feared to take their part he would do it alone. After a last effort to persuade them he became silent, and spent one whole day by himself in solitude and prayer. When the early morning came the clergy sent to call him as usual to matins. They looked for him in vain; he was nowhere to be found. The sacramental cup was also gone, and the book which he used at the Holy Communion. He must have stolen away in the darkness, and gone to face by himself the danger which they dared not share. Then they found out how much they loved him. They knew where he must have gone; they were filled with fear for him and shame for themselves; they went after him in haste and forced him to come back. Next morning they started in company with him, and crossed the gulf by ship to Stettin.

The danger was not in fact so great as they had supposed. Several occurrences had already taken place at Stettin to prepare the people for their coming, and help to turn the tide. The multitude were ready to see a miracle in everything; and more than once it had seemed to them that the hand of God was visibly put forth to give glory to the Name of Christ. One of these events had occurred on the day when they had rushed wildly to pull down the Christian church. One person had been particularly forward in the work of destruction. He snatched a hammer and ran before the rest to have the glory of striking the first blow. He mounted a ladder and lifted his weapon to strike. But an unexpected blow fell upon himself. His hand was paralyzed; the hammer dropped from his hold; he himself fell fainting from the ladder to the ground. The strange God was defending His temple; would it not be wise to give up the rash effort at destruction, to leave the Church standing in its beauty, to build around it altars to the ancient gods, that all alike might receive the honour and worship which were their due? So the stricken man advised; so the multitude determined to act; so perhaps a rude, uncultivated crowd were certain to interpret what had happened. There is nothing improbable in the story. The conflict of contending impulses, faith and unbelief, superstition and fear, might well have palsied the hand with terror at such a crisis, without any exceptional interference of supernatural power.

But another and mightier influence was at work. Among the more cultivated inhabitants of Stettin there was one of some consideration and mark who had the courage to speak his mind, and who was openly bearing testimony to the kingdom of Christ. Wittstock was his name. He had been converted and baptized by Otto at his former visit to the town, and the seed which had then been sown in his heart had so far taken vigorous root that it was impossible for him to return to the idol-worship. He was lured onwards by a gleam of real light, and though dim and distant still, it was the sure promise of the dawn. Otto's courageous faith and confidence in God, his self-denying love and steadfast will, had made an impression upon him which was not to be effaced, and he groped falteringly towards the same ideal. From the day of his conversion he had invariably refused to take part in any warlike enterprise against Christian people. To this extent he recognized that he had become a member of a brotherhood; but against heathen he still considered that it was lawful, if not meritorious, to wage war.

He had lately taken part in a plundering expedition, apparently against the inhabitants of that very Isle of Rugen where Otto wished so much to preach the Gospel. He had been taken prisoner, and put in chains. In this period of enforced quiet his thoughts turned inward, and he found a support in prayer and meditation. Once he had been praying long and earnestly and afterwards fell asleep. In a dream he saw Bishop Otto coming to him and assuring him that his prayer was heard; he should soon be delivered from his confinement and restored to his home. Very soon after this dream an opportunity of escape actually offered itself. Contriving to free himself from his chains he slipped unobserved to the sea shore to take whatever chance might exist of leaving the island. An empty boat was at the water's edge, and none were near. No time was to be lost. He leaped into the boat, and without oar or sail committed himself to the mercy of the waves. A gentle breeze sprang up from the North and helped him on his way; a short voyage brought him back to Stettin.

His own belief was that he had been set free by a miracle, and guided across the waters by supernatural aid. He had the boat hung up publicly at the gate of Stettin as a lasting memorial of the heavenly interposition. "This boat," he afterwards said to Otto, "is a witness to your holiness which had power with God, it is a confirmation of my faith in Christ, it is a proof and pledge that He Himself has sent me to preach the Gospel to this people." From that time onward he devoted himself to his work, bearing fearless testimony to the power and mercy of the Redeemer, and warning those who had fallen from the faith that they were cutting themselves off from everlasting life.

Such things as these had prepared men's minds for the arrival of the Bishop, and when Otto came his commanding presence was sure to have its full effect. But he himself knew nothing of all this; he had heard only of the wild fury of the multitude, and he entered the city determined to do the work which God had so evidently marked out for him, but with a heart prepared for martyrdom.

But it never was his custom wantonly to aggravate the dangers of his path, or to rush without a cause to an unprofitable death. He entered the city with prudent caution, and took refuge first in a church which stood at the gate. Here he determined to pause with his companions, and form a plan of action when he had learned more accurately how matters stood within the city. But his coming was immediately known; and the heathen priests, already furious at the work which Wittstock was doing, were resolved that the Bishop should not escape them. The church should be razed to the ground, and all within it should perish. But calm courage and a steadfast will had their usual effect upon the frantic fury of the multitude. Otto committed himself and his friends to God in prayer, and then walked out of the church arrayed in his episcopal robes; the cross was borne before him, and the clergy were around him, chanting psalms and hymns. The crowd were confounded at his courage and the little account which he took of their fury. The priests found themselves powerless. There was a dead silence. At last the crowd dispersed. Not a hand had been laid upon the Bishop. Otto and his clergy were left alone. This was Friday; Otto knew that his work was only begun, by no means finished; he spent the Saturday in prayer and fasting.

The same day Wittstock, never backward in speaking out whatever was in his heart, became bolder than ever, and went up and down continually among the people, preaching to them of the vanity of their idols, and proclaiming the irresistible kingdom of Christ. Now and again he returned to the Bishop, bringing with him some friend or kinsman for his blessing, declaring over and over again his conviction that all would be well, and consulting what next should be done.

When Sunday came he received the Holy Communion with others at Otto's hands, and then all in a body made their way to the market-place. Here there was a pulpit from which the magistrates were in the habit of addressing the people on public occasions. A multitude was already assembled round it. Otto mounted the steps and began to preach. Very few showed any inclination to interrupt him, and the vast majority of the crowd were listening with respectful silence to his words. It was evident that unless the spell were broken he would speedily carry the people with him. Suddenly his voice was drowned by a loud cry and continued shouts of defiance. One of the heathen priests, a man of gigantic stature and immense bodily power, was forcing his way through the crowd, arrayed in his priestly robes, and calling upon his countrymen to take this opportunity of avenging the outraged honour of their gods. What more acceptable offering upon their altars than the life of the Christian bishop? His words had their effect. Numbers seized their weapons and poised their lances to hurl them upon Otto. He stood unmoved, and not a weapon was thrown. Like the lions round

Daniel, the multitude were awed by some mysterious influence which they could not resist. They felt that there must be an unseen presence supporting his calm composure and fearless courage; they recognized the strength of a spiritual power to which they were not accustomed. Once more the fury of the heathen priests was baffled by an invisible enemy, and the setting sun which was to have witnessed the murder of the Bishop saw men bowing down before him as a manifest messenger from heaven.

Next day there was a mass meeting held to decide over again the great question of the worship of the gods. From break of day till midnight one after another rose and spoke. The issue was certain. One after another declared that the courage, the strength, the love, the gentleness of the Bishop were not of this world. The kingdom which he preached must be indeed the kingdom of God. He swayed them by the majesty of the spirit which shone in his life. At length at midnight a decree was passed that the idols should be utterly destroyed, and that throughout the land men should give glory to the name of Christ.

Wittstock had taken an active and prominent part in the debate; he had spoken long and spoken strongly; and his own force of character and well-known earnestness of purpose had added force to his words. He hailed the decree of the assembly as the final victory of Christ in the land. Overflowing with gladness, he could not wait till the morning light, but ran at once to tell the Bishop what things had been done. It was a night much to be remembered in Pomerania. Early in the morning Otto rose, and called his clergy together to celebrate the Holy Communion, and render high thanksgiving to God for the victory of His grace. Then he called a meeting of the people of the place. He had much to say to them. A great blow had been struck, and a great victory had been won; but it was the beginning, not the end of the struggle. They must not be content with submitting to baptism, and naming themselves by the name of Christ. The door of their hearts must be thrown open before Him that He might enter in and take possession of all their lives. He spoke to hearts already deeply stirred by all that had lately passed, and ready to receive the impression of his words; and the mark which he made that morning was not soon nor easily effaced. The first result was, that numbers of those who had fallen away, and whose lukewarmness had caused the revival of idolatry, now came forward begging humbly to be restored to the communion of the Church. They received free forgiveness for the past, and earnest warnings to fight the battle of Christ in the future without fear or shame.

Otto's personal labours in Pomerania were now nearly at an end. He was still Bishop of Bamberg, and he could not be much longer absent from his own diocese; but his work was by no means complete. The voice of the multitude had declared for Christ, but the voice of a multitude is a fickle and a changing thing. How many hearts were burning with love of the Crucified? How many would grow lukewarm again, or cold when the first excitement had subsided? There were many, too, who had taken no part in the decree which welcomed the messengers of the Gospel; many who were still heathen not only in heart, but in outward profession, and who were roused by the late events to more deadly hatred than ever. Otto's life was safe now from public violence, but many times he ran extremest risk of death from assassination or secret assault. Nor were the attempts at murder always secret. As he was leaving Stettin to sail down the Haff to Julin the heathen party gathered together to make a last effort to destroy him; but he seemed to bear a charmed life, or rather a special Providence seemed to watch over him; no weapon raised against him prospered; and he escaped out of their hands.

Julin, as before, followed the example of Stettin. The idols were destroyed; the churches rose. Otto began once more to turn longing eyes westward, toward the Isle of Rugen. That island was still a stronghold of the prince of darkness; if he could but win it for Christ and spread the light of the Gospel there! As things were then, it would be almost certain death for him to land on such a shore; but he was never wanting in courage, and he would have welcomed joyfully the crown of martyrdom.

But he was wanted at home, and he must leave Pomerania never again to return. Light and darkness were struggling in Germany in even a more confused and bewildering conflict than on the shores of the Baltic. Otto had been the friend of Henry IV., with whom Pope Gregory VII. had waged such deadly war. Both Pope and Emperor had passed away from this world, but the great battle had not ceased. It was a time of perplexity and doubt, when the best of men found it difficult to see their way. The Apostle of Pomerania would bring to the discussion of ecclesiastical disputes and the settlement of civil discord the keener insight and the wider view which he had gained in the simpler conflict with idolatry in heathen lands.

In the year 1128 he made a tour among the churches which he had founded in Pomerania, and then finally returned to Germany to play what part he could in the Imperial Diet. The missionary labours of his life were over now. Only by messages and presents he showed his undying interest in the people among whom he had suffered and done so much.

Nearly half a century afterwards King Waldemar of Denmark succeeded in subduing the barbarous inhabitants of the Isle of Rugen. The idols were destroyed by the conquerors, the lands belonging to the temples were seized for the support of the clergy, and Rugen called itself Christian at last.

Similarly, by force of arms, the standard of the Cross was extended along the southern shore of the Baltic, eastward of Pomerania. Men were compelled by violence to submit to baptism and to call themselves Christians. An order of spiritual knights, called the Brotherhood of the Soldiers of Christ, was formed for this express purpose. In this way Livonia was subdued about the year 1200, but it was not till nearly half a century again had passed that Prussia, about 1240, named itself by the name of Christ.

We have seen how the spirit of Missions gradually changed in the course of centuries. St. Patrick planted the Gospel in Ireland in a manner resembling that in which the Apostles had preached it, relying upon its own power to commend itself to every man's conscience in the sight of God. St. Boniface leaned much upon the protection of princes. Anschar shielded himself with the sacred character of an ambassador, and the message of the Gospel was delivered under the shelter afforded by the message of the civil power. Otto was supported by an armed force to control by strength of arms the violence of the heathen multitude. We have seen how earnestly he desired to stand without this earthly prop, but circumstances and the spirit of the age seemed to render it impossible. At last the spirit of the Crusades took full possession of men's minds; and, though gentler means were not forgotten, it was by violence and the sword alone that they oftenest expected to extend the Church of Christ.

Was it indeed the Gospel which was preached in such a manner? Could the message of the peace of God find its way by such means to the hearts of men? We only know that it is written that the wrath of man shall turn to His praise; and, looking at these things in the light of later events, we can see how the soil so broken up has afterwards yielded an abundant harvest; and North Germany, which received the cup of living water so strangely mixed with the poison of men's earthly passions, has herself in her turn held forth the Word of life to the nations.

THE END.

LONDON:
GILBERT AND RIVINGTON, PRINTERS,
ST. JOHN'S SQUARE.

PUBLICATIONS
OF THE
Society for Promoting Christian Knowledge.

Most of these Works may be had in ornamental bindings, with gilt edges, at a small extra charge.

	Price. s. d.
ADELBERT AND BASTEL. A Story for Children. Translated from the German by permission of the Author. 18mo. cloth boards	1 0
A JOURNAL OF THE PLAGUE YEAR. Being Observations, or Memorials, of the most remarkable Occurrences, as well Public as Private, which happened in London during the last great Visitation in 1665. Written by a Citizen who continued all the while in London. Imp. 16mo. cloth boards	3 0
A THOUSAND YEARS; OR, THE MISSIONARY CENTRES OF THE MIDDLE AGES. By the Rev. JOHN WYSE. (Cat. G. XVII.) On toned paper, with four illustrations. Crown 8vo. cloth boards	2 6
BATTLE WORTH FIGHTING, THE; and other Stories. Fcp. 8vo. cloth boards	2 0
BUTTERFLIES AND FAIRIES. Royal 16mo.	2 0
CASTLE CORNET; OR, THE ISLANDS' TROUBLES IN THE TROUBLOUS TIMES. A Story of the Channel Islands. By LOUISA HAWTREY. With four illustrations on toned paper. Crown 8vo. cl. bds.	2 0
CHARLEY ASHLEY. The Adventures of an Orphan Boy. With six full-page illustrations on toned paper. By J. G. WALKER, Esq. Crown 8vo. cloth boards	1 6
CHRISTIAN FATHERS, THE. Lives of Ignatius, Polycarp, Justin, Irenæus, Cyprian, Athanasius, Hilary, Basil, Gregory Nazianzen, Ambrose, Jerome, Chrysostom, Augustine, Gregory the Great, Bede, and Bernard. By the Rev. G. G. PERRY, M.A. Post 8vo. cloth boards	3 6
CHURCH OF ENGLAND BIOGRAPHIES. Hooker—Usher—Herbert—Leighton—Lady Falkland—Jeremy Taylor—Ken—Margaret Godolphin—John Newton. Crown 8vo. with four Portraits, cloth boards	2 0
CHURCH OF ENGLAND BIOGRAPHIES. Second Series. Wilson—Hannah More—Joshua Watson—Legh Richmond—Heber—Blomfield—Dr. Scoresby—Longley—	

PUBLICATIONS OF THE SOCIETY.

	Price.
	s. d.
CLEAR SHINING AFTER RAIN. (For Girls.) By Mrs. CAREY BROCK. Crown 8vo. cloth boards	3 0
CYCLE OF LIFE, THE: a Book of Poems for Young and Old, Town and Country. Printed on toned paper, illustrated with eighteen woodcuts, handsomely bound in cloth, gilt edges, bevelled boards, fcp. 4to.	7 6
EARTH'S MANY VOICES. First and Second Series. With illustrations on toned paper. Royal 16mo. extra cloth, gilt edges ....each	2 0
The two series in one volume	4 0
FISHES, FAMILIAR HISTORY OF BRITISH. By FRANK BUCKLAND, Inspector of Salmon Fisheries for England and Wales, &c. &c. With numerous illustrations. Crown 8vo. cloth boards...	5 0
GOLDEN GORSE; AND UNCLE MARK'S SNOWBALLS. By FLORENCE WILFORD. With three illustrations on toned paper. Crown 8vo. cloth boards......	1 6
GROSSETESTE, THE LIFE AND TIMES OF ROBERT, BISHOP OF LINCOLN. By the Rev. G. G. PERRY, M.A. Post 8vo. cloth boards	2 6
HARRY WATERS AND JOHN HEARD, a Lesson from the Field; or, Like Seed Like Fruit. Crown 8vo.	2 0
HATTY AND NELLIE; OR, TWO MARRIAGES: A Story of Middle Class Life. By Mrs. CAREY BROCK. Crown 8vo. cloth boards...	2 6
KING'S NAMESAKE, THE: A Tale of Carisbrooke Castle. Crown 8vo. cloth boards	2 0
LIFE OF BISHOP PATTESON, SKETCH OF THE. (Cat. G. XVII.) With four illustrations on toned paper. Crown 8vo. cloth boards...	3 6
LING BANK COTTAGE: A TALE FOR WORKING GIRLS. With two illustrations on toned paper. Crown 8vo. cloth boards	2 0
LIONEL'S REVENGE; or, The Young Royalists. Fcp. 8vo. cloth boards...	2 0
MARION; OR, THE SMUGGLER'S WIFE. With four full-page illustrations on toned paper. Crown 8vo. cloth boards	2 0
MARY: A TALE OF HUMBLE LIFE. (Cat. G. XVII.) With three illustrations on toned paper. Crown 8vo. cloth boards	2 0
MAYS OF LORTON, THE. A Tale of Village Life. 18mo. cloth boards	1 6
MEG'S PRIMROSES, AND OTHER STORIES. Royal 16mo. cloth boards	2 0
MESSAGE, THE; AND OTHER STORIES. With

PUBLICATIONS OF THE SOCIETY.

	Price. s. d.
NATURAL HISTORY OF THE BIBLE, THE. By the Rev. H. B. TRISTRAM, M.A., F.L.S.	7 0
NEW STORIES ON OLD SUBJECTS. (Cat. G. XVII.) By C. E. BOWEN, Author of "Stories on my Duty towards God and my Neighbour," &c. With four full-page illustrations on toned paper. Crown 8vo. cloth boards	3 0
NURSE MARGARET'S TWO ST. SYLVESTER EVES. (For Girls.) A Tale. Translated from the German by OTTILIE WILDERMUTH. Royal 16mo. paper boards	0 8
PANELLED HOUSE, THE. A Chronicle of Two Sisters' Lives. By M. BRAMSTON	3 0
PARABLES OF LIFE. (Cat. G. XVII.) By the Author of "Earth's Many Voices." Royal 16mo. on toned paper, with seven illustrations. Cloth boards, gilt edges............	2 0
RIGHT WAY AND THE WRONG WAY, THE; OR, THE ARDINGLEY LADS. By A. R. N., Author of "Woodbury Farm," "Margaret Vere," &c. With three full-page illustrations on toned paper. Crown 8vo. cloth boards	1 6
RINA CLIFFE. (For Girls.) A Village Character. By E. M. L. With three full-page illustrations on toned paper. Crown 8vo. cloth boards	2 0
SANDWICH ISLANDS AND THEIR PEOPLE, THE. By M. A. DONNE, Author of "Denmark and its People," &c. Fcp. 8vo. cloth boards.............................	2 0
SCENES IN THE EAST. Consisting of Twelve Coloured Photographic Views of Places mentioned in the Bible, beautifully executed. With descriptive Letterpress, by the Rev. H. B. TRISTRAM, M.A., LL.D., F.R.S., &c., Author of "The Land of Israel," &c. &c. 4to. cloth, bevelled boards, gilt edges	7 0
SCHOOL AND HOLIDAYS. A description of German Upper Class Life. (For Girls.) Translated from the German. With three illustrations on toned paper. Fcp. 8vo. cl. bds.	1 6
SELBORNE, THE NATURAL HISTORY OF. By the Rev. GILBERT WHITE, A.M., Fellow of Oriel College, Oxford. Arranged for Young Persons. New Edition. Cloth boards	3 0
SHORT READINGS ON THE APOSTLES' AND NICENE CREEDS. (Cat. G. I.) By the Rev. JOHN ASTON WHITLOCK, M.A., Vicar of Leigh, Surrey, Author of "Short Readings on Portions of the Litany," &c. With Notes and References. Demy 16mo. cloth boards............	1 6
SILENT JIM; a Cornish Story. By JAMES F. COBB, Esq., Author of "A Tale of Two Brothers." With four full-page illustrations on toned paper. Cloth boards	3 0

PUBLICATIONS OF THE SOCIETY.

	Price. s. d.
ST. CEDD'S CROSS. A tale of the Conversion of the East Saxons. By Rev. E. CUTTS. Fcap. 8vo. cl. gilt edges	2 6
STORIES FOR EVERY SUNDAY IN THE CHRISTIAN YEAR. Fcp. 8vo. cloth boards........................	2 0
STORIES OF SUCCESS, as illustrated by the lives of humble men who have made themselves great. By JAMES F. COBB, Esq., Author of "Silent Jim." With four illustrations on toned paper. Crown 8vo. cloth boards	3 0
STORIES ON "MY DUTY TOWARDS GOD." Crown 8vo. cloth boards...	1 6
STORIES ON "MY DUTY TOWARDS MY NEIGHBOUR." Crown 8vo. cloth boards..................	1 6
STRANGER THAN FICTION. (Cat. G. XVII.) A Story of Mission Life. By the Rev. J. J. HALCOMBE, M.A. With eight full-page illustrations on toned paper. Post 8vo. cloth boards	2 6
THE SEA KINGS OF THE MEDITERRANEAN. By the Rev. G. FYLER TOWNSEND, M.A., Vicar of St. Michael's, Burleigh Street, Strand, Chaplain to the Corps of Commissionaires, &c. With four illustrations on toned paper. Cloth boards...	3 0
THE TOPOGRAPHY OF THE HOLY LAND; OR, THE PLACES, RIVERS, AND MOUNTAINS MENTIONED IN THE BIBLE. By the Rev. H. B. TRISTRAM, M.A., LL.D., F.R.S. Crown 8vo. cloth boards	4 0
THE VILLAGE BEECH-TREE; OR, WORK AND TRUST. With four page illustrations on toned paper. Crown 8vo. cloth boards..	3 0
TO SAN FRANCISCO AND BACK. By a LONDON PARSON. With numerous illustrations. Crown 8vo. cl. bds.	2 6
UNCLE TOM'S STORIES; OR, BUZZES FROM INSECT LAND	1 6
WANDERER, THE. (For Boys.) By Mrs. PEARLESS (late ANNE PRATT). Crown 8vo. with three full-page illustrations, cloth boards	2 0
WHAT FRIENDS ARE MEANT FOR. With four illustrations, on toned paper. Royal 16mo. cloth boards...	1 6
WINTER IN THE ARCTIC AND SUMMER IN THE ANTARCTIC REGIONS. By C. TOMLINSON. With two Maps. Crown 8vo. cloth boards	4 0
WRECK OF THE OSPREY, THE: A STORY FOR BOYS. Fcp. 8vo. cloth boards	1 6

Depositories:
77, GREAT QUEEN STREET, LINCOLN'S INN FIELDS, W.C.
4, ROYAL EXCHANGE, E.C.; 48, PICCADILLY, W.;

www.ingramcontent.com/pod-product-compliance
Lightning Source LLC
Chambersburg PA
CBHW021404230426
43666CB00006B/636